From Mormon to Mermaid

One Woman's Voyage from Oppression to Freedom

A Memoir by Lorelei

First Published
2016

Murmuring Rocks Publishing

ISBN-13:978-159011422
ISBN-10:1539011429

Printed in the United States of America

Cover design by Marie Blair

Author photograph by Ryan Michael Brewer

Dedicated to strong women unafraid to stand alone.

A symbol of transformation,
mermaids whisper from the sea—
Live true to your inner heartstrings,
and your truth will set you free.

ACKNOWLEDGMENTS

"You should write a book," my friend told me after I shared some of my former Mormon beliefs with him years ago. "You could call it, *Mormonism to Mermaidism.*"

Good idea.

Since that night, many have been there for me as I've written my way through *From Mormon to Mermaid.*

I would like to thank all the friends who read early drafts and pushed me to continue, friends in the Wordsmiths critique group who fostered me, and friends in the California Writers Club who continue to support me. I also wish to thank Randy Lee Eickhoff who helped edit my work, Marie Blair who designed my cover, and, of course, my friends who lived their own stories, and also left the Mormon Church.

A big thanks to all of you, my friends.

Contents

From Mormon to Mermaid

One Woman's Voyage from
Oppression to Freedom

Born into a devout Mormon family—and named after a mermaid—
a woman searches through tangles of Mormon doctrine
to discover that the deepest truths lie within.

ONE

THE LORELEI
1944

*T*he young sergeant fixes his eyes straight ahead, desperate to make sense of the scene before him.

If only it would move closer, he thinks, riveted to the spot. *There it goes again. What kind of crazy tricks are my eyes playing on me?*

He stands alone on the jagged shoreline. He draws in a deep breath of cold Mediterranean Sea air and shoves his hands deeper into his worn army-issue jacket, trying to clear his head. Far to his right loom threatening cliffs, and in the distance fog hangs over the choppy sea, but it's the waves close to the rocky ledge near his feet that command his full attention.

Again, there's uproar in the waters. He tries in vain to determine the source of the disturbance just as something leaps high out of the waves.

Did I really see something green flip up? No, that's impossible. I'm so damn lonely, I'm fantasizing.

After all, fighting in the Second World War on the other side of the world could muck up anyone's head.

Yes, he rationalizes, *I'm missing home so much, especially missing her, that I'm imagining things.*

He turns away, but a murmuring sound grabs his attention and he jerks back around just as the waters bubble up with life. *Splash!* His eyes chase the bubble trail left behind as something bursts through the surface, flips high in the air, and sprays sea foam all over his face. His fingers trace the salty wetness on his rough-shaven cheek. He gasps at the wonder of her as she continues whirling and spinning, revealing her glistening breasts, waist, and hips, which taper down to an out-rageously green . . . tail!

She continues diving in and out of the water, the bubble jewels in her red hair gleaming in the last beams of the low-hanging sun. He can't escape the pull of her sultry smile, her skin all shiny from the salty sea, or her long hair flowing down and caressing her mother-of-pearl thighs.

His mind reels in confusion. Rumors had swirled through his platoon of Lorelei, the mermaid who perched on a rock in the Rhine River and lured sailors into danger with her singing, but never in his maddest dreams had he considered her more than a legend, or that she might rove from river to sea. At least, not until now.

Her red hair, dripping in seashell fragments, triggers both intrigue and frustration. It reminds him of another redhead, thousands of isolating waves away. How he aches to be with his new bride. He misses her creamy pale skin, her innocent touch, and her arousing aroma.

He closes his eyes, remembering the last time they were together back in the States. When he opens them moments later, the water lies placid, a single ripple dancing across the surface. The air hangs heavy with sea scent as his mind spins with questions. Could the siren really exist? His finger touches the dripping splat-ters still on his face, and the assuring wetness makes him smile.

The memory sticks fast in my father's mind throughout the rest of the war, along with the memory of her name—Lorelei.

Not many years later, I climb up on his lap, place my arms around his neck and ask, "Daddy, how did you and Mommy choose my name?"

We settle back in his big chair. He puts his rough chin up close to my ear and shares the magical tale of the Lorelei.

"Oh no, Daddy!" I say, "You named me after a fish lady? A naked fish lady? How *could you* name me after a mermaid?" I feel a flush creep across my cheeks. After all, I've seen pictures of half-naked mermaids.

He grins, a distant look comes into his eyes, and I get no more out of him.

As I grow older, my embarrassment continues to rise as I see pictures of the Lorelei brimming with raw sexuality. I soon discover that mermaids are rarely, if ever, modest. Mormons aren't keen on being naked—my folks had taught me bet-ter than that. Even as a child, especially a good Mormon child, I know no good can come from all that "s" stuff—sex, sensuality, seduction.

My Mormon heritage runs deep. More than one hundred and fifty winters ago, my foremothers yoked themselves to the upstart new faith and bravely trudged behind pioneer husbands on the long trek across wind- and snow-driven plains to the valley of the Great Salt Lake.

My entrance to the valley, however, proved less dramatic, although I did arrive in Provo, Utah, naked and crying. That long-ago December day in 1946 brought a Christmas snow that swaddled in white the Brigham Young University campus where both my parents were students.

I'm standing in my daddy's boots in 1948.

A year and a half later, a baby brother joined our family, and we moved to Salt Lake City to live "under the shadow of the temple," as we said in hundreds of family prayers. The answer to one prayer arrived twelve years later when a baby sister showed up to complete our family.

I'm so Mormon, polygamists practically fall off my family tree—from long-ago great-grandparents to present-day cousins. Oh, the stories of polygamy I've heard as they trickle down through the generations from foremothers who lived that "divinely" harsh principle. Although the concept of multiple spouses has changed from how Joseph Smith started it, with most of the ramifications now shifted from this life to the next, in Mormon Town, polygamy still remains alive and sticking as a founding principle.

Growing up in the complicated doctrinal net called Mormonism, my parents taught me the basics—since I was a special spirit in heaven before I was born on Earth, God sent me to a faithful family of Latter-day Saints during these "last days." Ever since the Church's beginning in 1830, the end of the world has loomed prophetically overhead.

Church leaders heaped on the rest—the Garden of Eden was in Jackson County, Missouri, a group of Jews sailed from Jerusalem to the Americas in 600 BC to become the American Indians, and the Mormon male's ultimate reward is to become a god. Damn good news for the men! This god status entitles them to have many wives in heaven—just like their

Mormon god. But since I am a woman, my scenario is different. If I'm very good and obey all their rules, my ultimate reward will be to become *one* of those wives—as part of a goddess harem.

Surely that's heritage enough without being loosely related to a fish.

Why in starfish heaven did my father choose a legendary mermaid as my namesake? What possible insights could his little Mormon daughter ever gain from a mermaid? Did those dank waters whisper secrets of mystical wisdom? Share longings of nautical freedom?

Bound to her memory, could my father have tossed me a liberating line of freedom by choosing to name his firstborn daughter Lorelei?

Our family gathers by our Christmas tree in 1952.

We welcome my new baby sister in 1958.

TWO

HOOK, LINE, AND THINKER
1953

I grab my mother's hand for warmth as we hurry past the towering trees that dwarf the small brick homes lining our South Salt Lake street. In our rush to leave, I've forgotten my coat. Again. Even though Mom often sets our kitchen clock ahead to trick us into being on time, it hasn't worked this Sunday morning. But then, it rarely does.

The huge cottonwood trees shed rusted summer leaves helter-skelter in the crisp autumn air as birds overhead flap their way south. We rush on, soon entering a timeworn church that fits well into the older neighborhood it anchors.

We hymn, heed, and pray through Sunday school in the plain chapel, then split into classes. I skip up the linoleum-clad stairs to where our teacher waits for her chicks to gather round, her arms folded across her fluffy middle, her warm dark eyes welcoming us. I grab a metal folding chair as the other seven-year-olds bound pell-mell into the small room.

"Today," our teacher begins, propping a picture of our prophet against her ample chest, "we'll begin by singing one of our favorite songs, 'Follow the Prophet.' All together now."

Our voices ring out in assorted keys.

"Now, who knows what our lesson is about?" she asks.

Without even raising his hand, Fred-the-know-it-all whoops out, "Following the prophet!"

I glare at him because he's always pulling stuff like that. He didn't even raise his hand. I wish I had his kind of nerve to just call out. After all, I know the answer too. I'm just way too shy. But our teacher seems to like the suck-up, because she chuckles her approval.

She goes on, "And when we follow our prophet, we know how to live so our families can always be together."

I know I always want to be with my mommy and daddy. I even want my little brother to hang around us forever. Well, most of the time, anyway.

"Our prophet tells us what we have to do to live as a forever family," she continues, pointing to the picture. "So, boys and girls, that's why our leaders say, 'When the prophet speaks, the thinking is done.' Now, what should you remember from today's lesson?"

"Follow the prophet!" Fred shouts again.

What a show-off.

I'm glad the prophet leads our church, but does that means he talks to God? I think I'll ask my daddy.

When class is over, I'm happy to leave Fred behind as I head to the foyer to hunt down my little brother. It doesn't take long to spot Mom's trademark red hair and Dad's familiar balding head. Mom's the prettiest lady at church, and for sure Dad's the smartest. Mom tells me she married him because he could answer all her questions, so when I grow up, I want to marry a man who knows everything too. Just like my daddy.

After finding them, I entwine my fingers in Dad's waiting hand as we join the tide of people flowing through the church's exterior doors as if a levee broke—twelve-year-old boys who have just passed the sacrament, teenage girls wearing modest-length skirts, a white-haired man wobbling on his cane and holding up the exodus, and a group of middle-aged women too busy visiting to care.

Once we're outside, my question flies right out of my mouth. "Daddy, since the prophet leads our church, does he get to talk to God?"

A grin makes its way across my father's face. Talking about Church doctrine is his place to shine, and goodness knows he has few enough of those. Although Dad graduated from Brigham Young University with a bachelor's degree in sociology, things just haven't gone well for him career-wise. Money has always been scarce. But despite his financial shortcomings, he still knows the answers to all my questions.

I jump two big steps to catch up.

"Listen," he says, giving my mom a quick wink. "Yes, our prophet receives revelation from God. That's one thing that makes our church so special, having a prophet to lead us."

"And my teacher said, 'When the prophet speaks, the thinking is done.'"

"That's right, honey. If we make good choices and follow our prophet, we'll be able to live with God one day."

"And we get to choose, huh Daddy," I say as I skip alongside him. "You said so."

"Yes, we do. And the biggest, most important choice we make, is deciding to follow the prophet. When we choose to follow him, we are still using our free will to always do what he tells us. It doesn't mean we don't keep asking questions and learning, but like your teacher said, once our prophet speaks, 'the thinking is done.'"

I look up at him as we continue walking. A brisk breeze flaps up my Sunday dress, plays with my mom's hemline, knocks about my father's big tie, and sniffs at my brother's smaller one. Their plain dark ties flop gleefully, defiantly even, against their mandated white shirts. And as we walk toward home, only a block from our Mormon chapel, like most homes in Salt Lake, I think about what my teacher said about following the prophet, what my daddy said about our choosing to follow the prophet. I think about it with every step as the gusty wind plays with my Sunday clothes, because one thing's for sure—my daddy knows the answers to all my questions.

Dad fills our acre lot and its untamed mass of greenery with chickens, rabbits, and a belligerent turkey or two. My little brother and I rotate weeks feeding the critters. When the weather freezes, I break the ice from the rabbits' bowls to fill them with fresh water, and on sunny days, I watch the bright sun shine on the iridescent black and rich red feathers of the cackling hens.

I feel sorry for those chickens though, because I know just as soon as they get big and fat after pecking up the chicken feed I scatter, they're headed for the Sunday soup. They're easy to make pals with, too—much easier than those kids at school. These feathered friends don't care if my clothes come from a musty thrift store, or if Mom cuts my bangs crooked, and they would never bug me about being skinny. Here in the backyard, I'm the boss. I'm important. Heck, I'm even brave at new introductions. I stoop down and pet a hen that comes close by me, but she doesn't put up with it for long. She just clucks offs, scraping her scaly feet into the soft dirt as if she has something better to do than entertain me.

My brother and I watch the chickens in 1954.

I wonder about those chickens and rabbits. I mean, how do they fit into the eternal scheme of things? Daddy has explained it all to me about the purpose of life and how I need to make good choices so God will be happy. Do the rabbits have to make good choices too? Does God care about their velvety white fur or flaming pink eyes? As I open one of the cages and dig my hand into the food sack, I lock eyes with a big white buck.

I fill his feeder, then stroke his soft back and ask, "What's it like, being a rabbit?" His whiskers twitch in silent response. "Daddy says we chose everything about our lives here on Earth before we were born. Did you get to choose, Mr. Bunny? And did you choose to be a rabbit? Or would you have rather been a chicken?"

I'm pretty sure the answer must be in the scriptures someplace. Daddy should know.

At our house, everything centers on the gospel. Our family prays together, stays together, and studies the Book of Mormon together. Some years down the road, Dad will write a book on his beloved Book of Mormon scripture, corralling the whole family into contributing.

But we seldom study the Bible, because we know that the *pure* truth, the *free-from-translation-error-and-direct-from-God* truth, exists in the Book of Mormon. We believe poor translations limit the biblical truth, as Joseph Smith explained in number eight of his thirteen Articles of Faith: "We believe the Bible to be the word of God as far as it is translated correctly; we also believe the Book of Mormon to be the word of God."

My dad and gospel discussions go together like sand and seashells. Our home may be poor in buying shoes or shirts, but it's rich in family discussions about God, truth, and the saving principles of Mormonism. All the important stuff.

In fact, Thought and Logic enter our humble home as honored guests like dolphins gliding in ocean waters. The huge tank of Mormon doctrine in our home gives these guests a perfect place to leap and swim.

Thought is the free-spirited one of these two aquatic sidekicks. He splashes into action any time a school of new ideas swims by, turning and twisting to get a better look at things. He can be silly or sensible, play in the edge of a swirling idea, or splatter new thoughts around just to tease.

Logic, on the other hand, is all business. Things simply must make sense or all halibut will break loose. As I grow older, however, the herrings will scatter and swim for their lives as I begin to grapple with the host of problematic claims by Mormon prophets.

Mormons gather each April and October in Temple Square's big Tabernacle to hear the prophet speak at General Conference. As our small family steps inside the historic building, the strains of organ music and the rich smell of old wood greet us. They remind us of the long-ago pioneer ancestors who built the Tabernacle.

As we sit on the hard benches, we can almost hear the whispers of those foregone craftsmen who labored carving the wooden pews and tying the rafters tight with pieces of green rawhide. Sitting there surrounded by our heritage and eager to hear counsel from God's top reps, I proudly join the congregation in raising my right hand to sustain silver-haired David O. McKay as the ninth Prophet, Seer and Revelator of the Church of Jesus Christ of Latter-day Saints.

If my dolphin companions Thought and Logic join me at these Mormon conferences, will they insist I think for myself instead of parroting,

"When the prophet speaks, the thinking is done?" And if we stay close pals through the years, will they keep me swimming near the shores of Mormonism? Or will they chart me a different course and help me pioneer a new way of living under the sun, sand, and sea?

THREE

DAM THAT EQUALITY
1958

Streaks of soft orange fabric fly past my eyes, followed by a blur of pale blue. Music from the radio fills the room as Mom and I whip our scarves through the air, then let them fall as gently as jellyfish floating in calm sea waters. Mom's arms twist gracefully above her red hair as the green scarf floats in arcs around her body.

"Move your body high, then fall to the floor," she explains. "And watch how I hold my hands." She touches her thumb and middle finger together as she swishes her wrists back and forth. They look like two small birds fluttering in a sea breeze, trailing the scarves behind them.

"Wheeeee!" I whoop.

"Now, move fast, then slow," she says. "Contrast adds interest."

I try to imitate her graceful moves, which she remembers from modern dance classes at Brigham Young University, so maybe one day I can dance like she does.

We twirl and twist around the cramped living room, letting our scarves fly, two Isadora Duncans dancing together.

Living at our house, you never quite know what to expect.

Yesterday when I got home from school, art projects lay strewn around the living room. Once again, Mom had given neighborhood kids art lessons. The smell of turpentine hung crisply in the air, and bright splashes of oil-based colors on pieces of irregular cardboard shapes lay drying underneath the piano bench. Tubes of paint and bunches of brushes lay scattered on an old copy of a Salt Lake newspaper across the coffee table. All amid the perpetual clutter we call home.

I found her out back kneeling next to a mound of dirt she smoothed with a shovel, her cheeks smudged with soil. In answer to my puzzled look, she motioned a gloved hand to a nearby heap of bricks.

"I want to clear an area and set in those old bricks the neighbors gave us so we'll have a little patio in our jungle, away from the chicken coops."

I nodded, yet wondered how she planned to turn the chaos of uneven ground and waist-high weeds under old gnarled apple trees into a patio. That pile from the neighbor would go only so far. I've learned Mom's creativity runs wild and that organization often gives up trying to keep pace.

But how I loved the giraffe Halloween costume she made me back in third grade by remodeling a fur coat she had tracked down at a thrift store. Her creative juices always flowed best under pressure of a deadline, meaning she finished past the deadline, which also meant I scrambled into my class-room late. When our class joined the marching parade through the school, I struggled to steer the giraffe's bulky body between the narrow rows of desks. Peeking through eyeholes in its spotted neck, I pulled ropes to open and close the mouth in its papier-mâché head. I'll never forget how my teacher and friends gushed over my furry, long-necked costume.

My brother joined the parade as a giant plum. Mom had made the plum head by covering a big balloon with strips of wet newspaper, letting it dry, cutting eye holes, and painting it purple. Then she attached the big green and yellow variegated leaves she designed to float over his green shirt and pants.

The chaotic kitchen with its pots overflowing with paste and strips of newspaper strewn around seemed a small price to pay for such creations.

And what other kid on the block has a mom who paints a fresh-cut watermelon on the kitchen floor because the old linoleum has worn through to the gray boards beneath it?

Yep, things are different at our house. I've gotten used to it, because with a mom like mine around, the place overflows with creative projects. My mom's a redhead and an artist. I figure that explains a lot.

Mom's musical creativity reigns supreme in our home too. Most of her projects aren't too outlandish, but when they involve me, they can be exas-perating. Like when Mom ropes us all into entering a talent show in our Mormon ward, which is what we call our Mormon congregations.

Mom makes my brother and me fantastic
Halloween costumes in 1954.

"It will be fun," she announces as we're eating dinner. "We'll sing 'The Orchestra Song,' and we'll each sing like we're a different instrument while we pretend to play them."

Lisa grins a giant grin. But she's too little to realize how mortifying it will be for us all to be on the stage singing as a family.

"We'll be awful!" I cry, dropping my fork.

"We'll all have a part. Jason, you can be the drum . . ."

"I don't want to!" my brother wails.

"Lisa, you can be the clarinet . . ."

Lisa's naïve grin is plastered on her face.

"... and we'll need a violin, trumpet, and horn," Mom continues to her captive audience.

"Please, dear ..." my father starts to say.

In the end, of course, Mom gets her way. She usually does. When the big day comes, at her insistence, we add theatrical touches by elbowing each other out of the way to get to the mike for our instrument's solo. The family member who gets pushed pretends to be aghast but continues drumming or violinning away. The audience roars. In the last verse of the song, we join together, singing and playing, to form the orchestra. We clarinet, horn, trumpet, and sing our hearts out. It turns out we're pretty good after all. And we have so much fun, we win first place in the ward competition. We then go on to compete on for our whole stake, a peculiar Mormon term meaning a group of five or six wards. Hallelujah and pass the swordfish, we win first place there, too.

When road show time rolls around, a musical production each ward churns out every other year, it's a given that my brother and I will audition for parts. Pulling off these road shows takes the talents of most of the teens who jump at the chance to be on stage, but balk at rehearsals, and are pushed along by the enthusiasm of most of the adults who write the scripts and direct the action.

On opening night, an amateur stagehand whisks back the red velvet curtain and flips on the bright floodlights, and we all bask in our twelve minutes of fame, just shy of the fifteen minutes Andy Warhol allots everyone. This performance takes place in front of all the members in our home ward. Then we hit the road with kids, costumes, and scenery in tow, taking our show to other wards.

Most of the road show finales I may forget, but not this one. Picture it: Stage lights flood over us, teenage girls in a chorus line linking elbows, stepping high and singing with gusto the theme song for our production, "It's a gentlemen's world that we live in, whether we are proud of it or not ... da da da da da ... da da da da da ... for we know it's a gentlemen's world."

These lyrics chuck creativity out the porthole as dogma floods in. This sets the stage not only for our road show but also for our place in the world. Indoctrination to a beat.

Everywhere I look, I find men in charge. Men anchor all the television news programs, lock down the main government positions, and command all the important Church callings. Even my father's foot is stuck in the man-is-superior bog, for as he explains to me, "As you know, honey, although most women cook, the great chefs are always men." Don't tell Julia Child!

So that's the way it works—it *is* a gentlemen's world. I figure it's just as well. The men lead and take care of us, and as long as we remain true to our faith, marry in the temple, and stay home with the children, God will protect us from the traumas of divorce or desertion. These bad things happen only to non-Mormons anyway. Since our husbands will always be there for us, it makes perfect sense for them to take charge.

Hold that thought.

During the coming decades, however, a threatening challenge will roar across the Utah Wasatch mountaintops—the radical idea of equal rights for women. Although the Equal Rights Amendment of the 1970s causes controversy all over the country, nowhere is the chant "Stop ERA" heard louder and clearer than in Salt Lake City, Utah.

Members opposed to equal rights debate its world-changing ramifications. Will the amendment force Boy Scout and Girl Scout troops to meet together? Require unisex bathrooms in malls and elementary schools? Or disallow altogether mother-daughter or father-son school events? Yet the big question is—how will gender equality impact the Mormon gentlemen's world?

The gentlemen in charge aren't taking any chances finding out. Uniting under the direction of our prophet Spencer W. Kimball, Church leaders join ranks regarding the amendment—all staunchly opposed. Our congregations unite in donating money against it, giving out literature against it, and railing over the pulpits against it. The gates guarding the Mormon gentlemen's world are closed, locked, and bolted against women clamoring for equal rights.

One way to deal with uppity women who have the nerve to suggest equal opportunity is to bar them from the workplace. Instead, keep them home embroidering pillowcases, playing the piano, or painting pictures for the living room. My mom's creative talents may be valued in their limited realm of family or Church, but not in the workplace for a boss who will pay her actual wages.

Although the Church encourages our feminine talents—such as road shows written or directed by women, children's visual aids created by a woman's hand, or ward bazaars with quilts composed of thousands of women's stitches—these creative expressions lie firmly under the thumbs of men wearing dark jackets with matching trousers.

Fifty years down the road, dark suits will still stand guard at the gates of the Mormon gentlemen's world as they shield the "holy grail" of male authority from all feminine influence. I'd love to believe equality for Mormon women blows in the wind, and if that ever happens, I would be the first to sign up for an all-woman chorus singing "Hallelujah Sister, Our Time Has Finally Come."

But in the meantime, I've figured out a few things. First, always vote for equality. And second, suits—either Mormon men in black coats, or bikini tops on mermaids—are entirely optional!

FOUR

SAND DOLLARS
1960

*C*link clink clink.

I pour my trove of hard-earned quarters and dimes into a shiny pile on my bedroom floor. The coins bounce on the old wood that I sometimes like to shine when I get ambitious and clean my room. Which won't be today. But my purring kitten, Catnip, who likes to sleep in my room, doesn't seem to mind. She's keeping me company curled up on a crumpled pile of clothes.

I open the white envelope and, one by one, push some of the coins inside.

I've worked hard for this money, chasing after my neighbor's four little kids. It's a hectic way for a fourteen-year-old to earn money, especially at the going rate of twenty-five cents an hour. But the first ten percent of anything I earn is sacred. I know how important paying tithing is "in the eternal scheme of things," as my father often says. Of course I'll give the Lord his part. I can't gyp God.

I invite my black-and-white fur ball into my lap and stroke her softness, which vibrates under my fingers, before sealing the envelope. I want it ready to give to my bishop first thing Sunday morning.

Every December during our Sunday Sacrament service, we can count on two holiday traditions. First, we'll sing our favorite Christmas hymns, and second, we'll hear the annual tithing lecture. Once again, the story of old will be retold how God revealed to the early Church leaders the principle of tithing to keep the Church afloat, and how paying an honest tithe heralds blessings beyond measure.

"If you pay the Lord first, you'll never go without," the speakers perpetually promise. They hang their sermon on a well-known Mormon scripture, "for he that is tithed shall not be burned at his coming." (*Doctrine & Covenants* 64:23). Because of this, we affectionately refer to tithing as fire insurance.

As devout Mormons, we believe paying a full tithing brings God's richest blessings, in both this life and the next. In this life we can enter the temple and be married for eternity, and in the next we can step through Mormon's version of the pearly gates, the highest heaven, called the Celestial Kingdom. Only full-tithe payers receive God's promise to live with their family in this glorious place. Because I want to live with my mom and dad forever, as soon as my tithing envelope jingles full of coins, I hand it over to Bishop Bergman.

Life in our home hinges on living the "gospel plan"—the beliefs of Mormonism—even though our family's finances are stretched as taut as iron straps binding a sea chest. But we always pay our tithing.

Back when my dad was still a student at Brigham Young University, a kind neighbor left milk on our doorstep once a week because she knew our family couldn't afford such a luxury. Years later, my mom would tell me the story to share the importance of thanking people. She confided in me that even though the milk meant so much, living in such need caused her to be too embarrassed to say thank you if she passed the neighbor on the street. Soon, the milk stopped.

Milk or no milk, however, my parents always paid their tithing.

My birthday falls exactly one week before Christmas, and before my tenth one, Dad offered me a choice. "I have a deal for you. This year you can either invite friends to a birthday party, or I'll put five dollars into a college fund for you. What do you think?"

Curly ribbons on presents and lighted candles on a cake didn't stand a chance in such a contest—I knew the importance of education, so I chose the money. But birthday party or not, we always pay our tithing.

Hand-me-downs and secondhand are second nature, but we always pay our tithing.

Dad goes behind supermarkets after dark to find thrown-out food. I slice off the mold from the tamales he brings home and let the chickens cluck over those mildewed chunks. The rest we serve for dinner. And we always pay our tithing.

Dad impresses us with the importance of a college education along with the importance of earning a scholarship to help defray the costs. Mom suggests ideas for essays and critiques my poetry. Dad works with me through tough algebra assignments and insists I sign up for Journalism. I join the high school newspaper staff and I'm named editor for my senior year, which will mean lots of work, but it's a great addition for my scholarship application.

Our efforts pan out. My brother and I will both be awarded full-tuition scholarships to BYU, Mom and Dad's alma mater. Priorities in our home are crystal clear: pinch pennies, work for scholarship, and always pay our tithing.

During my high school years, our old water heater often goes on the fritz and refuses to supply us our daily hot water. Washing dishes or taking a bath is complicated when we must heat water on the kitchen stove, then haul it to the sink or bathroom.

"Jason," I shout to my younger brother. "Help me get this kettle from the stove so I can fill the tub."

He begrudgingly agrees. It's not a fun job, but I need to take a bath. Once I've roped him into helping, we grab hold of the kettle and lift it from the stove. We struggle toward the bathtub as the steam rises into our faces. I take one halting step forward, and he follows, lugging the kettle of boiling water between us. Through the living room, into the small hallway, and into the bathroom. Almost there. Now the trickiest part—we must lift it up and over the side of the tub. But his fingers slip, we lose our grip, and the scalding liquid tips back and pours down the front of my jeans.

"Yee-ow!" I shriek. The blinding pain sears as the scalding water burns down my legs, forming giant puddles of pain on my feet. Mom rushes me into the car, and Dad screeches our old black Plymouth out of the driveway in his mad dash to get me to the hospital emergency room, where the doctor announces I have second- and third-degree burns over my legs and feet.

For weeks, the burns ooze serum through the gauze bandages taped around my swollen feet, which causes me to miss school and hobble like a one-legged pirate for months. There's no money for my folks to replace our worn-out water heater, but we always pay our tithing.

Like all good Mormons, we believe in fasting because weakening the body brings us closer to the spirit of God and shows Him our humility. The first Sunday of each month is Fast Sunday, which means we give up food and water for two meals and donate that money to help needy members. Since no one would believe how little we spend on food, Dad feels he must ratchet up the amount we pay for our fast offering. And we always pay our tithing.

We "put our shoulder to the wheel," like the title of a favorite Mormon hymn, to push the welfare program along. Mom and I volunteer together at the Church cannery on Welfare Square, located close to Temple Square in downtown Salt Lake City. Afterwards, we do a walking tour of the square and see the dairy plant, bakery, and the Church-owned thrift store, Deseret Industries. Dad explains to me the word "deseret" is a term used in the Book of Mormon which Joseph Smith translated as "honeybee," so to us the beehive stands for a symbol of industry and hard work.

As I stand next to the massive concrete grain elevator, I feel small. It's so big, it holds more than eighty tons of wheat. I'm proud to be part of all this. The Church also owns cattle ranches, farms, and canneries all over the United States. Not only do we contribute to this giant welfare system, but we also always pay our tithing.

When workers at Kennecott Copper go on strike, which puts my dad out of work for a summer, we apply to the Church for food. The canned goods we receive all have the Deseret Food logo on the label, which boasts a yellow beehive surrounded by buzzing worker bees—but this food in bright packages is not a handout. Because my dad started painting houses as a sideline while a student at Brigham Young University, the bishop makes an offer: If Dad will paint the entire church house, he'll give us food. My father, who would remain devout all his life, later would comment to me, "The Church sure got the best of that deal." But we always pay our tithing.

When December rolls around, Dad selects a time slot from the roster on the bishop's door and signs up for our family to meet with the bishop for annual Tithing Settlement. My parents must pay their tithing in full by the end of the year to receive their Temple Recommends. Without these recommends, they cannot attend the temple to ensure their place in the Celestial Kingdom.

The bishop sits behind his large wooden desk holding the receipts that show our family's yearly contributions and asks, "Is this your full tithing for this year?"

"Yes," we can always answer as we sit across from him on metal folding chairs, because we always pay our tithing.

Before school on chilly winter mornings, my brother and I hover over the floor furnace for warmth. Years later, the old furnace will catch fire and burn half of my parents' home. They can't live there amidst charred walls, but while the insurance company makes slow repairs, where can they go?

Mom and Dad stand in their fire-ravaged home.

Dad's only option is to pitch a tent in the backyard where Mom's non-kitchen consists of a small refrigerator running on an extension cord from the neighbor. Do Church members rally and show up with standard Mormon green bean casseroles or green Jell-O? No. Does the bishop extend any offers of help? No.

Mom and Dad survive in that tent the whole summer. Their faces age ten years. But they always pay their tithing.

By then I'm a newlywed living in California. One Sunday morning, our bishop requests everyone come to a special meeting that night, so I drive to the chapel alone, as my husband no longer attends church.

"The Church is constructing a new building," Bishop Adler explains, standing erect at the pulpit in the chapel, "and we need you to step up and help. We have prayed to know the amount God wants each family to donate."

At the conclusion of the meeting, he hands everyone an envelope with the individual God-inspired figure written inside. As I sit in the pew by myself, I hesitate before I tear open my envelope and peek in. Two hundred dollars! This is a heavy chunk of money for us, especially when it's in addition to the ten percent tithing *and* five percent budget we already pay. At the end of the meeting, I move slowly out to the foyer.

I decide to level with him about my dilemma. "I know my husband won't like this. In fact, the only way I can pay it is if I don't say anything."

Bishop Adler doesn't respond, so I ask him straight out, "Should I talk to my husband, or just pay the two hundred dollars without telling him?"

His inspiration comes in a flash. "Write out the check."

If I could look ahead, I'd see the woman I'd become would be ashamed I'd even ask such a question. Ashamed I'd put the advice of my bishop first, hand my bishop a check, and never tell my husband. But after all, the Church comes first.

And we always pay our tithing.

In our family, the tradition of paying tithing is as strong as the moon's gravitational pull on the ocean. Take my grandfather's example. On January 20, 1968, at age eighty-three, he went to his bishop's office to attend yearly tithing settlement. He received his Statement of Contributions, which shows the amounts he contributed to the Church of Jesus Christ of Latter-day Saints that year:

Fast Offering Fund	$28.00
Missionary Fund	30.00
Welfare Fund	55.00
Building Fund	0.00
Budget Fund	60.00
Other Fund	5.00
Tithing Fund	1,236.36
Total Contribution	$1,414.36

Mormons have opportunities galore to contribute to the Kingdom. My grandparents sacrificed to pay their ten percent tithing—plus all the other funds listed above—to qualify for the streets of Mormon heaven. Although his receipt would have you think his income for that year totaled $12,363.60 (ten times $1,236.36), that was just what my grandpa would *want* you to think. As my father explained, "Grandpa didn't want his bishop to know how poor they were. So he paid lots of extra tithing."

Always poor, always proud. And he always paid his tithing.

The Mormon Church headquarters nestles in the mountains of Utah, where Mormon prophets speak of all nations flowing unto Zion (aka Utah), and lots of shiny things flow into Salt Lake City. In fact, it would take a sea chest the size of the *Titanic* to hold all the gold coins that stream from faithful members across the world's oceans and fill their coffers.

This commitment from generations of children, parents, and grandparents to pay their tithes and offerings to the Lord to secure their forever family status makes the Mormon Church one of the richest churches in America. Not to mention one of the biggest corporations, because you can be sure the Mormon Church always collects—instead of pays—its tithing.

FIVE

ANCHOR OF FAITH
1951 - 1965

*H*eave, ho!

Shouting warnings of gale-force winds and waves, sailors band together and drop anchor, sending it plummeting through the brine to lodge deep in the ocean floor. The taut anchor line keeps their vessel standing firm against any blasting storm.

Religious rituals also anchor people's faith. For our family, one such ritual means visiting the block in downtown Salt Lake City known as Temple Square.

I'm five!

Fifteen-foot-high walls surround the manicured grounds. It may be Saturday, but since we're on Temple Square, there are no jeans or t-shirts for us. Dad wears his Sunday suit. Mom and I wear the matching emerald green dresses she made us. She holds three-year-old Jason's hand as I skip ahead past the domed Tabernacle, home of the famous Mormon Tabernacle Choir.

But it's our huge Salt Lake Temple I want to see.

"Our pioneer ancestors labored forty years to build it," Dad tells us. "They blasted the quartz monzonite, similar to granite, out of Little Cottonwood Canyon twenty miles away and hauled the blocks to the town center by oxcart."

Mom's artistic ability shines in her oil painting
of the Salt Lake Temple in 1944.

This isn't the reason the temple is so special, though. It's where Mom and Dad got married "for time and all eternity," which means our family will be together forever and ever. That special kind of marriage can only happen in a Mormon temple. I know I'll be married in a temple, and it will be the most important day in my life because that will be the day I'll begin my own forever family.

I'm eight!

I'm going to be baptized by my daddy today—right on my birthday, in the Tabernacle baptismal font, and right on Temple Square. To Mormons, eight is a milestone, the "age of accountability." Before my dad told me, I didn't even know there was a font in the Tabernacle. Every baptism I've gone to has been held in the small font in our ward building.

Our family enters through a rear door of the Tabernacle, and we step down a short stairway into the basement. The big rectangular baptismal font stretches wide in front of us.

Lots of dads are there to baptize their sons or daughters, and lots of moms sit on the side with the rest of their families. When my brother grows up, he can baptize his children, and when I grow up, I can watch my husband baptize mine.

After a short service, Dad leads me into the blue-tiled font. The water ripples around my waist, smelling fresh and clean. In just a few minutes, I'll be sparkly fresh and clean, too. At least for a day.

I hold my daddy's left arm, pinch my nose shut, and close my eyes. He raises his right arm to form a square and says the prescribed baptismal prayer. Then he drops me backward into the water and washes away all my eight years of nefarious sins.

When I break through the surface of the water, with the first breath I take, I'm a brand- spanking-new member of the Church of Jesus Christ of Latter-day Saints.

I'm nine!

My family and I enter through the large wrought-iron gates on the temple grounds for General Conference. We're here to listen to the counsel of our leaders, the Twelve Apostles, and our prophet.

Every seat in the Tabernacle and nearby Assembly Hall is already full, so we find a spot on the crowded temple grounds between fragrant dogwood trees choking with white blossoms and scented flowerbeds exploding with multicolored tulips.

After conference, we hurry to the back of the Tabernacle, hoping to get a glimpse of our silver-haired prophet, David O. McKay. But as he exits the building, a large crowd of followers gathers around him, blocking our view.

I hang close behind Jason as he makes his way through the crowd. He pops out the front, next to the prophet's black limousine. As the prophet shakes a few hands, Jason sticks up his small one, hoping to seize this once-in-a-lifetime opportunity. The prophet shakes it, but Jason wants more.

"Please, would you shake my sister's hand too?" he pleads, as he pulls me forward from the crowd.

The prophet smiles at Jason, then shakes my hand. Jason beams.

I'm eleven!

Our bishop "calls" me to play the piano for the children in junior Sunday school. Even though I'm not really that good on the piano keys—or maybe because of it—I'm offered the opportunity of six organ lessons at the big Tabernacle on Temple Square.

Each Saturday morning, Dad drives me downtown to the Tabernacle for my class. It's held in the basement, not far from the large baptismal font where I got baptized. The organ we practice on boasts three keyboards and a full row of foot pedals, quite unlike the piano I practice on at home.

Our older-than-Methuselah instructor sits at the organ and plays a rousing hymn to inspire us.

"The keyboards give melody and harmony, and the bass pedal notes add richness," he tells us as his old-slippered feet move with precision across the bass pedals.

A giant hook baited with opportunity dangles in front of us—the promise that during our last class, we will each get to play one hymn on the famous Tabernacle organ. It's one of the world's largest and most distinctive organs and sits right above us on the main floor of the Tabernacle.

When the big day arrives, a boy named Brent goes first. He's only a couple of years older than I am, but his fingers fly over the manuals as both his feet flick madly back and forth over the foot pedals. Just my luck to follow his kind of performance.

Although I've long given up hopes of conquering those pedals, I climb up on the wooden bench and face the massive organ. I gingerly place my hands on the center of the five manuals, ignore the hundreds of ivory-clad stops, and take a deep breath. Each chord I play reverberates throughout the giant Tabernacle, swirling around pillars and pews. I feel a kinship with all those who have ever played this organ, as well as all the generations of Mormons who have gathered before me in this giant Tabernacle to sing hymns of praise.

I'm twelve!

I'm going to the temple to perform a special ceremony—baptism for the dead. These proxy baptisms give people a second chance. If they somehow missed the missionaries knocking on their door in this life, they still have a chance to become a Mormon in the next.

"Shh," the white-haired temple worker keeps telling us as she chaperons our large group. We all had to wait until we're at least twelve because that's the age when the boys get the priesthood. Then, even without the priesthood, the girls can come too. We all head to the lower level of the temple, which symbolizes death and burial, and all change into white clothes.

We enter the baptistery through twelve arches. I draw in a quick breath as I take in the grandeur. It's clear that despite heart-aching poverty, my pioneer ancestors gave their best for their God. I soon figure that one of the perks of being dead is where you get baptized. This font knocks the sardines off the modest one where I got baptized four years ago.

Before us stand twelve life-sized golden oxen, in a circle facing outward, with non-seeing golden eyes. The oxen represent the twelve tribes of Israel. They're beautifully sculptured animals, but I feel sorry for them because their blank eyes are obviously blind. On their hefty haunches rests a six-by-ten-foot oval golden baptismal font, inspired by the Old Testament's Temple of Solomon.

"Keep it quiet," we hear over and over. Girls go to the left, boys to the right. We march in line to the long bench and wait our turn. I try to focus on the elegance surrounding me, but after sitting in silence for so long, I get bored. I invent a game of "footsy patty cake," with a friend next to me to pass the time. Our game soon has us snickering quietly.

A voice blazes from on high. "You're in the house of God!" the white-haired officiator by the font booms, stopping the whole ceremony. "You *must* be reverent."

Deflated like a blowfish targeted by stingrays, I hang my head in shame, appalled at my blasphemy. I've not only broken the silence—I've broken the rule. Will my sin cause God to reject the baptisms I'm about to perform?

When the officiator motions to me, I inch up the railed staircase leading to the top of the font. I wait my turn, then step down into the tepid water. As I slog over to the officiator, I don't dare look him in the eye. Thank goodness, he doesn't seem to recognize me as the rebel.

He begins to offer the baptismal prayer.

"Sister [my full name as the female proxy], having authority, I baptize you, for and in behalf of [name of dead female], who is dead, in the name of the Father, and of the Son, and of the Holy Ghost, Amen."

He tips me back into the water twenty times, each time inserting another name. These people aren't my friends or relatives, but their names were submitted by Church members anxious to offer them the baptismal blessings of Mormonism.

Two men, always men, stand as witnesses at the edge of the font and watch to make sure no renegade toes, feet, or hands pop up out of the water. If that happens, we'll have to do it all over again. Immersion, after all, means all body parts go under the water, just as John the Baptist baptized Jesus in the River Jordan. As Mormons, we don't go for the sprinkling thing.

When we finish, I clutch my water-soaked clothes, wrap a dry towel around myself, and hurry into the women's dressing room. Because I've completed the first part of this temple work, twenty dead people now have the chance to become Mormons.

On a later date on the temple's upper levels, Mormons will perform other phases of temple work for these dead—including marriage to their spouse. Announcements are not sent out to relatives about these sealings, nor are there tiers of wedding cakes announcing the vows of couples sealed by happy Mormon proxies.

We can only hope the couples so joined in eternal wedlock still like each other.

This practice of baptizing dead relatives, celebrities, and others will stir controversy among nonmembers, especially after word escapes that Mormons performed proxy baptisms for Buddha—and "Mrs. Buddha"—Gandhi, Adolph Hitler, Joseph Stalin, Elvis Presley, and Anne Frank, to name a few. Particularly offended will be the Jews, when they discover that proxies in Mormon temples baptized some 380,000 ancestors who died in the holocaust.

Despite apologies from the Church and a public promise to be made in 1995 to stop the baptisms without written permission, the baptisms will still continue. The controversy will rage on with no solution in sight, as devout Mormons feel the obligation to share the belief of making families eternal. And how do they do this? By baptizing as many of the earth's population as possible, living or dead.

I'm fourteen!

It's pretty cool to sit in these red-velvet seats where the famous Tabernacle Choir usually sit. Hundreds of girls all around me fill the rest of the seats, our eyes all fixed on our conductor. She's helping us memorize the words to the Mormon pioneer hymn, "They, the Builders of the Nation," for a dramatic reading. It's all part of the big festivities coming up to celebrate July 24, Pioneer Day.

On this day in 1847, Brigham Young led the Mormon pioneers into the Salt Lake Valley after they were chased out of Nauvoo, Illinois. Their non-Mormon neighbors wanted nothing to do with a people who married their teenage daughters to old men who practiced polygamy. These and other difficulties culminated in the great trek west.

Utah celebrates July 24 with a passion. It's an official holiday, filled with pageants, rodeos, reenactments, parades, and big and noisy fireworks for which celebrations of July 4 pale in comparison.

"Above all," our conductor tells us, "speak loud and clear, and always keep your eyes on me." As we continue, my voice rings out with the best of them. Then, to test that everyone is really watching, she cues an unexpected stop.

Oh no. I'm not watching closely enough, and my voice rings out all by myself. Everyone turns and stares at me.

Not missing a beat, she announces, "Thank you very much for that demonstration. See girls, disasters like this happen if you don't watch me."

At her reassurance, I take a deep breath. Life is worth living after all.

I use my babysitting money to buy the mandated Simplicity pattern and polished-cotton peach fabric. Then my mom joins hundreds of moms all over Salt Lake who sew up a storm of matching dresses. When the time for our performance arrives, the multiple side and rear entrances of the Tabernacle swing open, and hundreds of young girls step through each door reciting lines in unison, flowing up through the aisles like waves of peach foam.

I'm fifteen!

Our family braves a frost-covered Temple Square to see the spectacular Christmas light display, to hear the Tabernacle Choir's recorded carols, and to stand enchanted before the huge nativity figures. This year I'm holding tightly to the hand of my three-year-old blonde, curly-headed sister, Lisa. Our breath turns white in the night air, we wish each other Merry Christmas, and Dad reminds us about the importance of the birth of Jesus Christ, our Savior, who stands at the center of our faith.

We believe in Jesus Christ, in God the Father, and in the Holy Ghost.

And although we celebrate Jesus's birth on December 25 with the rest of Christianity, we know through Joseph Smith's revelations that Jesus was born in the springtime, on April 6.

We also believe Jesus Christ's conception occurred as a result of a natural union of the Virgin Mary and God the Father. In other words, Jesus's conception took place the same old-fashioned way yours and mine did. And no, Mary was no longer a virgin.

This belief, first declared by the second Mormon Prophet Brigham Young, was also validated by Apostle Bruce R. McConkie in his popular book *Mormon Doctrine:*

> God the Father is a perfected, glorified, holy Man, an immortal Personage. And Christ was born into the world as the literal Son of this Holy Being; he was born in the same personal, real, and literal sense that any mortal son is born to a mortal father. There is nothing figurative about his paternity; he was begotten, conceived and born in the normal and natural course of events, for he is the Son of God, and that designation means what it says. (p. 742)

This leads to some startling, although logical, Mormon conclusions, such as:

> Because God commands men and women to marry before having sex,
> and because God wouldn't break His own law,
> and because God had sex with Mary to produce Jesus Christ,
> God had previously married Mary—to obey His own laws,
> so God must have had another wife, who gave birth to people already on the Earth— including Mary—
> Therefore, God is a polygamist.

This gives us all a whole new understanding of the Christmas story.

I'm seventeen!

I walk arm-in-arm with my boyfriend on Temple Square. We sneak under the boughs of a huge pine tree to share a kiss within sight of the spires of the temple, the temple where I hope to one day get married. The snow-laden limbs hang down to the ground, completely hiding us. In this romantic secluded place, and while we share a kiss or two—okay, maybe a few more—

we manage to lose track of time.

A gruff voice abruptly knocks us out of our trance, demanding, "What do you think you're doing in there?"

A dog has sniffed us out. Make that a watchdog. A watchdog with a guard on the other end of his leash. Red-faced, and not just because of the cold, we beat it out of there.

Fast.

For decades, Temple Square served as an anchor tying my life to my Mormon beliefs—an anchor mooring me to my faith, to the truth of Mormonism, and to my forever family. Such an anchor could certainly withstand any tempestuous winds that might blow through my life.

Right?

I'm ready to start my senior year at
Granite High School in 1964.

SIX

A WORLD OF BLUE AND WHITE
1965

Our old Rambler lurches onto the freeway as Dad and I begin our forty-two-mile trip from South Salt Lake. My head's whirling with anticipation of the new life ahead of me, as long as this clunker of a car can get me there. Think of it, I'm finally a freshman at Brigham Young University. Whoo hoo!

Dad's unusually quiet this morning, even for him. But I imagine his mind swells with worries of costs not covered by my scholarship, such as housing, books, and food. Does this explain the growing bald spot on his head?

We drive along as the tires play a *whop-whop-whop* chorus on the pavement beneath us until Dad interrupts the rhythm by clearing his throat.

"I know you've worked hard for your grades and scholarship, hon, but you've got to be sure and keep it up." He glances over at me. "And the only way we can afford to have you attend BYU a second year, is for you to get your scholarship renewed. Do you understand?"

I hear the worry in his voice. "I know, Dad."

"It will take a lot of work," he says above the recurring *whop-whops,* "and I don't want you to ever look back and think, 'I should have studied harder.'"

"Yes, I know."

"Study hard—that's my best advice." He pats my knee.

I pull my focus from the rhythm of the tires and grin as I think of my mom's best advice. She came into my room last night just before going to bed, looking different without the red lipstick and makeup she always applied before leaving the house.

"I wear the brightest lipstick I can find," she had told me many times, "because redheads always need makeup. Otherwise I'd look washed out."

It's true her skin is pale, but a nice Mom pale.

She sat on the edge of my rumpled bed and confided, "You know, honey, always remember what's most important. You're going to BYU, the best place in the whole wide world to find a husband. A good husband. A good-returned-missionary-kind-of husband."

Got it, Mom. Find a man.

Got it, Dad. Study hard.

We exit the University Parkway off-ramp and head toward the BYU campus, which sprawls over five hundred acres at the foot of the Wasatch Mountains. Back to the campus where Dad and Mom met, back to the campus where I was born. Here I'll study long, get good grades, and pray hard to meet the One who'll take me to the temple. Although I may be one pale shell lying on the beach amongst hundreds of more flamboyant shells, with a hefty dose of God's help, I'm sure my future husband will pick me out.

He'll select me because of my sweet, spiritual nature, my faith in God, and my testimony of the Church. In my husband's eyes, I'll be beautiful. He'll be kind, want a large family, and be willing to work hard to take care of us. Will he have a dark complexion and hair like my high school sweetheart, Brian? I hope so. But Brian's Catholic, so as much as I've fallen for him, I know I can't marry him. And since I'm going to BYU, I realize it's time I put that high school romance behind me.

My Mormon husband and I will get married for time and all eternity, just like my parents, to start us down the road to matrimonial bliss. I'll cook the best meals, sew all our kids' clothes, and keep our house so clean, company could drop by any time. Mom, especially, will be impressed with my house-keeping skills.

Maybe in a few years, my husband will be called to be a bishop. I'll sit all proud in the congregation, flanked by our brood of five or six Mormon kids. All their faces will be sparkling clean. Each week, the boys will be wearing freshly ironed white shirts and the girls' hair will be brushed into shiny curls. I'll hold the new baby on my lap, yet manage to keep them all quiet while my husband's conducting Sacrament Meeting from the podium. Our life will be just about perfect.

I know eternity is a long time, so I'd better get this right.

I crank down my window, letting the autumn air with its scent of new beginnings blow through my hair. My fingertips thump on the windowsill, drumming the beat of BYU's fight song "Rise and Shout, the Cougars Are Out," while I picture the gyrations of our mascot, Cosmo the Cougar, at football games. And leaping through my head right beside him are members of the BYU's drill team's Cougarettes, decked out in our school colors of blue and white.

Just as blue ocean waves wearing foamy whitecaps curl themselves around the world, my expectations of BYU, which we call the Lord's university, wrap themselves around every hope and dream in my freshman head.

As we enter the campus, two monuments greet us, proclaiming the school's mottos on stone. On the left side we read "The World is Our Campus," and on the right side, "Enter to Learn—Go Forth to Serve." A new world, filled with new things to learn.

We wind our way to the student housing section of Wymount Terrace. Dad wrestles with my stuff-filled boxes, then helps me lug them up two flights of wrought-iron stairs to where my apartment and five other roommates wait.

As BYU students, we have all bound our souls to the Church with the promise to live by the Honor Code. I've signed the pledge that if I violate this code, it could cost me my diploma. In fact, if any of us leave the Church, we'll be in violation and would not be allowed to even continue to attend classes, much less graduate.

I know coffee and tea are strictly forbidden, so there will be no smell of hot morning coffee lingering in the dorms after long nights of studying at BYU. Also banned are beer, beards, and getting tattoos. Goatees, sideburns, and rolling joints. Cuss words, smokes, and poker chips. *Playboy,* bikinis, and skipping church. Sandals, shorts, and strapless tops. Form-fitting clothes and pants on girls. Above-the-knee skirts and sleeveless shirts.

The ultimate rule: *Do not have sex.*

My roommates and I soon share the chores of cooking and cleaning our small apartment, as well as commiserating over homework, heartthrobs and heartaches. Living with a bunch of other nineteen-year-olds is an eye-opener.

"Hello, Libby!" This busty roommate from England teaches us to say loo instead of bathroom, and we teach her why the cute guy in her English class looked at her askance when she asked him if she could borrow his rubber, her English term for eraser.

"Hello, Ava!" This nonchalant roommate exposes us to her love of nudity. As long as she's staying in, her clothes are staying off. *Shocking*. When she announces her mom's upcoming visit, we figure she'll zip up and button up. Not how it happens. We soon discover the source of Ava's proclivity as her mother prances around our apartment . . . just . . . as . . . naked.

"Hello, Marcy!" This roommate's dad is a physician in Spokane, and she teaches us that doctors get lots of free samples from pharmaceuticals. Her dad put them all in a box at their home, then whenever she would get a headache, her dad would tell her, "Go upstairs and look in the samples box for something." So much for doctor-tailored prescriptions.

"Hello, Beth!" She's so danged cute, all the guys follow her around like lost pearl divers. More than once when we are all at a dance and a guy discovers I'm her roommate, he asks me to dance to get an introduction. I wish I had a reflection as lovely as hers looking back at me in the mirror. I have little confidence around the guys Beth attracts with such ease. In fact, most guys look right past me, especially since I'm never brave enough to smile first. Beth teaches me what it feels like to be intimidated.

My scholarship is in journalism, and I discover I can't take even one writing class until the third year. I know I'll be lucky if my folks can afford two. When Beth tells me about the two-year business program she's enrolled in, I switch. Good thing Dad had insisted I enroll in a typing class at the LDS Business College in downtown Salt Lake two summers before. Although I had to take many rumbling bus rides to get there, the typewriter and I had immediately hit it off.

"Hello, JoAnne!" This down-to-earth roommate hits the wedding cake jackpot right off. On a Saturday night when she stays home with curlers in her hair, she answers the doorbell to let in Ted, who has a date with lovely Beth. The next day, Ted asks *JoAnne* out, and in two weeks, he proposes. Two months later, they get married.

Going to BYU is *the* choice for gals going after their "Mrs." degree, which affects the dating game. Guys don't even have to iron their own shirts, as girlfriends auditioning for wifehood routinely and happily set up their ironing boards and turn up the heat.

Since passing a Book of Mormon class is required for graduation, I sign up for this crucial class right away. Our leaders counsel us to read the Book of Mormon every day, and being a student at BYU makes this advice mandatory. My schedule announces that a popular and well-respected professor teaches the class, but when I peek through the doorway of the huge auditorium in the

Joseph Smith Building on the first day of class, I see long rows of more than two hundred seats in front of a large screen. Surprise—I've signed up for a film lecture course.

All any of us ever see of the revered professor is his image flickering on the screen in front of us. At the end of his films, there's no possibility of a question-and-answer period, no chance for interaction, no asking for clarification. Our place as students learning about the Book of Mormon is not to question or think, but to listen and obey—and to pass the class so we can graduate.

Although the lecture in front of me doesn't meet my expectations, a guy who takes the seat just behind mine exceeds them.

"Well, *hello*, Glen." His distinctions include being a returned missionary, or RM as we call them, being six-foot plus, having dark hair and being handsome to boot. Even better, he chose the seat right behind me on purpose. On our first date, he springs for a chocolate-drizzled sundae after church. How sweet it is.

"I'm from frozen Alaska," he tells me, but he looks pretty nice and warm to me. We talk about his mission, and he tells me how when he left, his girlfriend promised to wait for him. All missionary-standard stuff, right up until his twist—because when he flew off for his faraway mission port, he asked his girlfriend to wait for him *and live with his parents*. She moved in with his folks for the two years he was gone, which ensured she would still be waiting chaste and pure when he returned. After all, "going on a mission" and "Dear John" letters are a partnered cliché. His plan worked like a charm, at least for him. When he returned, his true love still waited, guarded under his parents' roof. Then *he* broke things off. After all, he was going off to BYU, where there were bluer seas to explore.

We don't last long. And I hate to admit it, but yes, I ironed his shirts.

I register for a first-year Spanish class, figuring with my two years of high school Spanish, I can keep my head above water. I fail to calculate that most of the other students in the class are returned missionaries who learned Spanish on their missions and are looking for an easy A. Almost half of BYU students serve missions. But I can keep up with a beginning Spanish class if I study hard, right?

Maybe not. Because our optimistic professor knows most of his students are returned missionaries, he teaches the class speaking only Español. His strings of south-of-the-border verbs whiz past me so fast, I *no comprendo* even our homework assignments.

When I catch him at his office to drop the class, he encourages me to stay, insisting, "You'll pick it up." I know if I don't drop the class, the only thing I'll pick up is a sure F. I drop out before I flunk out.

In my second year, I also honor a true BYU tradition and get engaged to a guy I hardly know. Well, I know the important thing—he is a returned missionary.

Yes, Mom, I remember your advice.

I'm glad Danny with the quick smile picked me. I'm also glad I'm thin or I might outweigh him, but he is nice and tall. We take off in his blue El Camino for a picnic, a standard BYU date, where he's asked me to bring the lunch so he can audit my cooking skills. *Humph!*

I think along the lines of golden fried chicken, and that's what I bring—in a red and white bucket featuring Colonel Sanders. Danny isn't impressed. After the picnic, he points to the trash cans on the far side of the park.

"You take our picnic trash over there," he insists as he sits on the grass. "That's women's work."

Now I'm not impressed.

The deal breaker? He wants to practice being married. No, it's not what you're thinking. "On Sunday," he insists as he squeezes my hand, "we won't kiss, hold hands, or even touch each other."

"Why not?" I ask, confused by his unromantic announcement.

"Because when we're married, we won't ever have sex on Sunday," he says, looking into my eyes, "and this way, we can practice living up to our upcoming sacrifice." Then he leans in for a soft kiss. It is Saturday, after all.

Now I'm even less impressed. I ask my mom what she thinks, and the expression on her face says it all. If our devout family hasn't heard of this sizzle killer, it must be some story made up by an old man with a low libido. Toodle-oo Danny.

My proudest success comes in Economics 101. Each Monday morning, my professor says, "Here's a pop quiz on this week's upcoming material." Each week, I fail. Luckily, these quizzes only assess our existing knowledge before the lectures and reading assignments, and don't count toward our grade. "But by Friday, you better know the material cold," he continues, "because that's the test that counts." I take copious notes, study like a sea demon, and, by the time the killer test comes each Friday, I hit the A high-water mark.

"No calculators allowed," says our professor as he stands in front of the tiered classroom in Accounting 101. I am often up at midnight, struggling to get the columns of figures to balance by hand, but they rarely do. I start the long problem over and if at 2 a.m. I still don't balance, I start over again. Because this class starts at 7 a.m., the crack of dawn, I often study all night, then show up at class feeling like a drunken tuna. If I were to use an illegal calculator, I might bump up my grade, plus gets some decent shut-eye, but I abide by the rules. At least I land a C.

Yes, Dad, I remember to study hard.

In 1966, BYU features Vice President Hubert Humphrey as a speaker. During this time, Utahans flurry about in one of their many end-of-time panics about food storage. Rumors wash through every street and down each alleyway that someone—the cousin of a friend's brother's neighbor's wife—actually *saw* the rationing tickets printed and soon to be issued by the United States government.

The rumors all confirm that staples such as sugar and flour will be rationed. Grocery stores all over the state sell record amounts of these staples. Like my family and friends, I spend part of my minimum-wage earnings from my summer job at Brown Floral on white enriched flour and pure cane sugar, which I store in five-gallon tins. Security in a can.

From the distance I sit from the podium, Vice President Humphrey looks just like another suit sitting in a long row of suits. At the end of his speech, some brave soul grabs his opportunity and shouts out in front of the huge crowd, "Why is the government printing rationing tickets?"

Taken by surprise, Vice President Humphrey insists, "The United States government is *not* planning to issue rationing tickets." His quick denial only fuels enthusiasm for the booming sales of the soon-to-be-rationed items. And like most rumors, when the rationing does not happen, the rumor drifts away into oblivion without explanation.

But back at our apartment, there's real news. In fact, it sizzles through my phone line all the way from Pope Air Force Base in North Carolina. My high school sweetheart Brian has found the Mormon missionaries, taken the plunge, and been baptized. This turned the former Catholic altar boy into a brand-new, full-fledged Mormon. Could this make all the difference for us?

A few months before I am to graduate in June of 1967, my phone rings again, this time with a request from a stranger asking me to play a piano solo at our commencement exercises. Who recommended me, or why, I haven't the foggiest idea. Although I'm flattered, I know I'm unqualified. But Mormons don't say no, which means I spend two months madly practicing a selection to play at my convocation exercises.

Then I wear my graduation gown and tassel with pride to accept my Associate of Science degree, and ride high on the crest of the BYU blue-and-white waves of celebration.

My diploma represents the many things I learned while living on the BYU campus, from literature to geology, quirks in roommates to Mormon-style dating. It also represents my commitment to bind my education, my life, and my future to Mormonism. Forever.

But there exists an undercurrent to the blue-and-white sea at BYU—one I know nothing about when I hurry across its magnificent campus for classes. This undercurrent swells with control and secrecy, instigated throughout the reign of our super-conservative president, Earnest L. Wilkinson. Although his twenty-year legacy includes an impressive increase in student enrollment and buildings on campus, it also includes firing professors who don't pay their full ten-percent tithing to the Church, organizing a student spy ring to expose any "pro-communist" professors, and supporting an extended electroshock-aversion therapy program to "cure" gays.

From a distance, team-spirited blue and white cover the world of my alma mater's campus, but beneath this placid exterior, embedded in layers of control, lie the forces that erode personal freedoms. "Enter to Learn," is the motto at BYU. And yes, I do learn many things while living on that Mormon campus, but more important are the things I don't learn. Things that stir and swirl, far down below the powerful, vast, blue-and-white sea.

SEVEN

SEAGULL'S LAMENT
1967

A howling wind swoops into the blue lagoon. Scooping up big gulps of water, it blows the wet mass spiraling high through an icy cloud that instantly transforms the droplets into bits of frosty flakes. Then, by command of whatever powers that be, on important days of my life, these frozen flakes drop in and cover my world.

They fell the December day I was born in Provo, Utah, and on another December day twenty-one years later in Salt Lake City. I remember more about the second winter day. The crystal flakes cover hillsides and homes in silence. Two stately evergreens standing as chaperones in front of a small Mormon church are soon covered with matching mantles of frosty stillness.

Inside the chapel's gymnasium, however, everything exudes hustle and hurry. Poinsettia reds and pine tree greens shout holiday cheer to helpful friends charging around the plain gym stringing lights and mixing punch. Candy cane centerpieces, twinkling white lights, and small round tables draped in white cloths complete the décor.

Free libido day! Or, said the old-fashioned way—my wedding day!

Everything brims with cheer except Doreen, my best friend and maid of honor, who looks simply uncomfortable. Her red velvet dress expands broadly across her midsection, but eight and a half months of pregnancy will do that to a midsection. I only hope her baby won't show up early. Her temple marriage was nine months ago, and she and her husband must be getting along.

Only three short weeks before this, I dialed her number, bursting to tell her my news. "Guess what, I'm getting married!"

"To Brian?" she teased.

"Of course Brian."

"But-but-but . . . what happened to waiting until he gets back from Vietnam . . . so you can marry in the temple forever?"

I hesitated. I had dreaded her asking this question but had known she would. I sat down on the couch, clutching the phone tightly.

"Don't you want to be with him forever?" she pushed. "If you get married in the chapel, you'll only be married for this lifetime. You need a temple marriage to have it last forever."

"It's just not that simple, Doreen."

Still, am I doing the right thing?

I slid further down in the cushions as my mind shot back five years before, to when it all started. On a busy Friday night, Doreen and I had giggled our way through the front door of Shakey's Pizza Parlor, modeling our bouffant hairdos, pegged jeans, and brown-and-white saddle oxfords. People had thronged around every table and huddled under clouds of wafting pizza scents as sounds of the Beach Boys "I Get Around" blared from the jukebox.

We had both spotted him right away, the cute-beyond-cute Italian guy behind the counter, wearing a flour-dusted apron. He tossed a pizza skin up in the air, sending it spiraling high to shoot off small bits of white powder on its climb, and then descend rapidly before crash-landing with a splat onto his upturned hand. Um um umm. And the pizza smelled good, too.

To her disappointment and my triumph, pizza boy asked *me* out, to see Dave Brubeck performing at the Terrace Ballroom, the largest in the country. I knew we could never get serious about each other since he was Catholic, but we still enjoyed the fun of pizzas, proms, and drive-in movies. Soon, he had begun talking about marriage, and about having six sons for a football team, and six daughters for a cheerleading squad. Didn't he know that a Catholic boy and a Mormon girl must go their separate ways?

After high school graduation, inevitably and heartbreakingly, it had to happen. In the fall, he had gone to Utah State and I had gone to BYU. When Vietnam heated up, he had joined the Air Force and flown off to boot camp.

But our whole seascape had changed when he'd called me at BYU and told me he had been baptized a Mormon, and we'd started our romance all over again.

Eight whirlwind months later, he popped the *big* question, which set up the whole problem. The Church requires a convert to be a member for one year before he or she can marry in the temple. We were four months short of forever.

Now I just hoped my girlfriend, and God, would understand.

"We wanted to wait, Doreen," I rushed to explain, "but the Air Force gave him a surprise Christmas leave before sending him overseas and when he came home for that whole month's leave in October it was sooooooooooo hard being good and now one more week together and oh golly what if we slip up and get carried away and end up in big trouble?"

I blurted it out, hoping to convince her. Or maybe I wanted to convince myself. Because the truth was—I liked it when Brian kissed me. I liked how it brought those sweet tingles bubbling all the way up from a new place deep inside, bringing breathy longings for more. I liked how the smell of his woodsy cologne mingled with my flowery perfume, and how his cheek felt rough next to my smooth one, especially when he held me real close. Which created the whole problem, of course, because I'd been taught that sex outside of marriage was the most serious sin I could commit, next to murder.

It's a harsh doctrine, yet I'd heard it many times over the pulpit. Joseph F. Smith, the sixth prophet of the Mormon Church, said, "We hold that sexual sin is second only to the shedding of innocent blood in the category of personal crimes." (*Gospel Doctrine*, 5th ed., pp. 309-310).

I knew that, "When the prophet speaks, the thinking is done." He spoke God's laws. My hormones may pump hard against it, but I must stifle my rebellious desires so I could be with my family in heaven.

God, please help me to be strong. Can Brian and I resist our sizzling feelings for another whole week and wait to get married in the temple when he comes back in a year? Even long kisses, necking, and petting were right up there beside the big sin, and if we got carried away, went too far, committed *the* sin next to murder, we wouldn't be able to get married in the temple. Only many more years down the line might the Church accept our repentance for such a huge mistake.

It would solve everything if the Church would loosen its policy grip and let us marry in the temple then. Dad insisted I make an appointment with our bishop and ask for an exception to the must-wait-one-year-after-baptism rule before a temple marriage. After all, this groom was a soldier going off to war. Dare I hope for a Christmas miracle?

I arrived early at the church and gave a nervous knock on Bishop Hardwick's door. Wearing a broad smile and an old suit, he opened the door and extended a warm handshake. He was the shortest man I had ever known. In fact, the only other adult I knew who was shorter was his wife. Guilt swept over me as I remembered that after their sixth baby was born, a girlfriend had whispered to me, "They're raising a generation of midgets!" I hoped he couldn't tell I laughed at such a joke.

Winter sunlight broke through a small elongated window above his desk as we settled into stiff wooden chairs, and I blurted out my dilemma.

"Bishop, Brian joined the Church eight months ago, almost a whole year, but he's going to Vietnam so could we please get permission to marry in the temple before he leaves?" I rushed on, unable to keep my nervous hands still on my lap. "We're worthy . . ." *Oh my gosh, we're not totally worthy, are we? I hope you won't suspect how tightly we push our bodies together when we kiss. Will you know?* ". . . and he's only four months short of being in the Church a year. But by the time his whole year is up, he'll be on the other side of the world in a war zone."

"No," he said, without hesitation. His smile faded and the expression in his eyes didn't flicker. "He must be in the Church one full year before he's allowed to enter the temple."

Time stalled. My eyes drifted up to the window high on the wall where I could see the weather outside changing.

"Lorelei," he continued, clasping his hands firmly together on his desk. "I must be clear. As your bishop, I can marry you here in the church building, but it won't be your real wedding. It will only last until you die."

I shifted in my chair, feeling uncomfortable. *I hope you can't tell how weak I am, how I melt into puddles of sensation when Brian holds me.*

"Your *real* wedding," he went on, "will take place in the temple after he returns home, where an officiator will seal you together for time and all eternity. If you marry now, outside of the temple, you know God won't recognize your marriage as eternal, and if while he's in Vietnam, anything should . . . happen . . ."

A sudden *rat-a-tat-tat* sound of hail pelting against the window startled me. My eyes darted up at the flurries on the outside pane. Icy whiteness filled the wind that would surround me on my walk home.

The bishop folded his arms across his chest, leaned back in his chair, and continued. "If you decide to marry now, although you can decorate the gym for your reception, strict rules must be obeyed regarding the chapel where I'll perform your marriage ceremony—no decorations, no ring ceremony, no "Here Comes the Bride" played on the organ, no having your father walk you down the aisle. Do you understand?"

I nodded. Of course I understood. *Why aren't I stronger? I should be pure like God wants me to be. If I were a better person, I could resist Brian's kisses instead of wavering, and I wouldn't even be here talking to you.*

There was nothing I could say. The rules were the rules, even during a war. I slowly stood to shake his hand before I turned to leave. I walked home against a chill wind that buffeted me with indecision.

Strong or weak . . . passion or policy . . . now or later . . .

God help me, I chose now.

Just six weeks to plan a wedding. The date, December 23, fell on a Saturday, two days before Christmas. Dad scheduled the church building for our reception, and Mom and I sped-shopped for red-velvet fabric and patterns for the bridesmaids' dresses. Although the bridesmaids would sew them, Mom said that if we cut all the dresses out ourselves, we could save money on fabric. We measured, we pinned, we cut. Mom talked Christmas tree lots into donating unsold trees to decorate the large gymnasium, and Dad strung white lights that twinkled against the green boughs.

I'm holding my poinsettia bouquet on my wedding day in 1967.

Are Mom and Dad disappointed with my choice? Will their status with their Mormon friends suffer because they lose bragging rights for a temple-married daughter? If so, they don't show it. They must know Brian and I are averting a potential disaster by marrying now.

Although Brian's Catholic parents don't exactly throw snowballs about their first-born son marrying a Mormon—those fights would come later—the whole Italian clan shows up for our wedding.

Portly Uncle Frank even comes without the bottle of booze he threatened to bring. The undecorated wooden pews in the bare chapel must look stark compared with the ornate Catholic church they attend, but they're in for a bigger affront from the bishop.

Bishop Hardwick stands before us on the podium, although it would take more than a podium to give him the illusion of normal height.

"Welcome, brothers and sisters," he begins, oblivious to the nonmembers seated in the pews in front of him. He continues our ceremony, giving counsel and quoting scriptures, but before pronouncing us man and wife, he rebukes all marriages conducted outside of Mormon temples. "Civil marriages, such as the one I'm performing now," he says, "are not eternal and only last until death. God is eternal, and therefore in God's eyes, only marriages solemnized in His temple are valid."

I cringe. *How must Brian's parents feel, hearing their marriage isn't valid before God? Will they be mad at me? Is this the place to preach our doctrine?*

But if Uncle Frank and the rest of the groom's Catholic family do an uncomfortable shuffle in their seat when they hear this, it's best they don't know the alternative. Outweighing the Mormon mantra of family first comes the restriction that nonmember parents, friends, and family are banned from the temple—even to attend a family wedding. If we had married in the temple, none of his family, even his parents, would have been allowed inside.

Outside, a frosty blur of flakes—inside, a frosty blur of dogma.

Our ceremony complete, we begin our six-day honeymoon with abandon. Then my new husband flies off to war, and after work I cry every night. For a whole year of hell, I wonder if the next day might bring horrific news. I can only write passionate letters, stuff them into perfumed envelopes, and airmail them off with a kiss.

Just before the next Christmas, the Air Force flies him back from Southeast Asia to San Francisco. Almost home. But when Brian calls me in Salt Lake, his "hello" sounds hollow. It's my only warning before he whispers his bombshell: "I don't want to be married."

"Brian, what?"

He hesitates. "I . . . don't want to be married."

"But why? You're finally home, and we can start our new life!"

"I don't know; I just don't."

Without further explanation, he hangs up the phone, leaving me whirling in confusion.

What's happened since you wrote your last passionate letter? Why have you turned our world upside down?

When his family and I meet him at the Salt Lake Airport, new Christmas snow covers the ground, but that isn't all that's cold. At his welcome-home party at his parents' home, I tell him I have rented a honeymoon suite in downtown Salt Lake City for his return, but he doesn't want to leave the large Italian clan who has gathered in his honor. He doesn't want to hold me. And when we get to the hotel, I find that's not all he doesn't want to do.

A white rock fireplace claims the focal point of our honeymoon suite, but there's no fire. For a very long time, he sits silently on the stone hearth by himself, and I realize I don't know this man at all.

Being passive won't solve this, only passion will. I entice him onto the bed and push myself into his arms. *I've waited so long for us to be together again. I love you . . . and you will love me . . . .*

If the words "I don't want to be married" were set to music, the refrain will become as haunting as the cry of a mournful seagull. I will hear it over and over and over again during the next twenty-four years.

And so we begin our marriage.

EIGHT

THE UNDERTOW OF UNDERWEAR
1969

*S*omehow, we've survived.

It's been over a whole year since Brian's come home from Vietnam and received his orders for the orange and sunshine state of California. Although we've come a long way from "I don't want to be married," it hasn't been easy.

Brian returned from Vietnam dragging duffel bags of anger and depression behind him. He never allows me to peek inside those bags nor shares with me any of their dark contents. And although the sound of a siren at night still wakes him in a cold sweat, he won't talk about any of it.

Struggling to decide what to do with his life, Brian uses the GI Bill to take general-course classes at San Bernardino Valley Junior College. He discovers the bow and arrow and joins the archery team. I work full time at Southern California Gas Company in Riverside and take some gourmet cooking classes.

Through it all, Brian is trying to learn the ropes of being a good Mormon. We go to church each Sunday morning and afternoon, accept callings to work with the youth organization each Tuesday evening, and attend Temple Preparation classes each Thursday evening. We pay our tithing, budget, and fast offerings. And there's always one more meeting to attend, scriptures to read, and talks to prepare.

God must be sitting astride His throne answering all my prayers, though, because, this sunny morning, this Monday morning blazing with promise for a new beginning, our yearlong challenges seem far behind us.

Over the weekend, we finally did it—we went to the Los Angeles Temple and were sealed for time and all eternity. We're *really* married.

As I hurry into work, I pause for a moment in front of the courtyard fountain and watch the splashing waters dance. The droplets seem to call out to me, "Work can wait. Come away—come and play." With a backward glance at the beckoning fountain, I fling open the large, plate-glass doors and rush into the lunchroom, looking for my new best friend, Patti.

The chatter of coworkers mixed with sizzling griddle smells and the pungent scent of coffee fill the air. I spot her right away in the far corner of the room, looking like the cover of a fashion magazine. She waves me over with one hand as she holds her morning coffee with the other.

I hurriedly grab a muffin before sitting down as I'm bubbling over with my exciting weekend news. But I don't get far before she interrupts.

"You have to wear special underwear?" she asks, tucking her long legs beneath her chair. "Are you kidding?"

"They're called garments," I correct, "and wearing them reminds us of our sacred promises—"

"And you wear them all the time, even now?"

"That's why my skirt is longer than yours," I explain, noticing her new spring mini skirt. "They're white, one piece, have cap sleeves, and come to my knees."

"So, this summer, you can't wear shorts or sleeveless blouses?"

"Well, no, because—"

"Or come to the beach with me?"

"I'd just change into my swimsuit once we got there," I say, scuffing my chair closer to the table.

But I don't tell her the waters at the beach are cursed, according to the revelations of Joseph Smith, which Mormons considered sacred scripture:

> Behold, I, the Lord, in the beginning blessed the waters; but in my last days, by the mouth of my servant John, I cursed the waters. Wherefore the days will come that no flesh shall be safe upon the waters. (*Doctrine and Covenants* 61:14-15)

This doctrine means Mormon missionaries aren't allowed to go swimming in any pools or beaches. But maybe I shouldn't go into that. Instead, it's time to turn the conversation to the perks of my Mormon underwear.

"The garments give special protection when we wear them," I venture, watching her eyes.

"Protection?" she asks, holding her coffee mug firmly in both hands and taking a quick sip.

Her raised eyebrows convince me to reconsider my strategy of sharing amazing garment stories, even though I grew up hearing them—stories like pioneers being spared by Indians if the natives got a glimpse of the garments, the faithful being shielded from fire where their garments covered their bodies, and members being protected against the tempting powers of the Evil One.

I hesitate, but her expression demands an answer as she sets down her cup and waits.

How can I explain this to someone who isn't Mormon?

"Yeah, protection, against all kinds of things . . ."

She says nothing, and I take the first bite of my bran muffin.

After a long pause, she asks the *big* question.

"What about sex? You must take your garments off for fun," she says, her brown eyes widening under her pixie bangs. "Even Mormons can't be that strict."

"Of course."

But please don't ask how Brian feels about wearing them. I'm supposed to be a good example for you so you'll see how happy Mormon couples are and join the Church.

"So, at least you guys can sleep together without them?"

"Well . . . we put them back on right after. For the rest of the night."

I really don't want to talk about this, but how do I get out of it?

"What?" Her eyes narrow. "You can't sleep naked with your husband? Why not?"

I scoot over to her to make sure no one can hear our conversation. "It's complicated," is all I can say. I figure that's better than saying, "We promised not to," or "God insists members of His true Church sleep with their special underwear on all night."

"No one would know if you don't put them back on," she says.

I begin chewing busily.

Sensing my uncomfortable hesitation, she pushes harder. "Come on, who'd know?"

"Well, in order to attend the temple, the bishop asks—"

"He *asks* you?"

I lean back in my chair and swallow hard. "Yes, he asks if we wear the garments day and night. And he means *all* night."

"But why would you even *answer* such a personal question?" she asks, forgetting to stir her morning addiction.

Years later, I'll ask myself the same thing. Why *did* I answer such questions? I'll also realize the price of my sacrifice not to sleep naked, breathlessly skin-to-skin next to my husband, every hugging moment of every hugging night.

But this morning, I simply answer, "I couldn't lie to my bishop."

The bustling noise of a workday anxious to start interrupts our conversation. I devour the rest of my muffin and shove my chair under the table, and we head back to the sales department.

There are too many things to try to explain over coffee and muffins. Not that I drink coffee, of course. I haven't even told her my new underwear represents the garment God made for Adam to cover his nakedness in the Garden of Eden, or that Joseph's coat of many colors is Biblical code for Mormon garments. These beliefs just might sound outlandish to a nonmember. In fact, some parts of my Mormon faith begin sounding strange even to me, especially as I try to explain them to a free-spirited soul like Patti.

Although we are best friends, our lives are polar opposites. While I have always followed the doing-what's-expected-of-me path, she hightailed it to Alaska right after she graduated from high school, searching for exciting times and a good-paying job. She found both. She knows what she wants and goes for it, or at least figures it out by the time she gets there. Oh yeah, I envy her daring nature, but I know one day she will regret not talking with those cute Mormon missionaries and joining up. And if she doesn't regret it in this life, well, for sure she will in the next.

Back at my desk, ringing phones and a busy workday clamor around me, contrasting sharply with the whispered quiet that enveloped Brian and me when we first entered the L.A. Mormon Temple early two mornings before.

"If you need to communicate, please whisper," a temple matron told us after we entered through the massive temple doors.

I followed a stooped senior attendant into the women's dressing area to change into the required all-white temple clothing. I donned my ankle-clinging, collarbone-concealing, wrist-tickling white temple dress. Then I approached a small white-curtained partition, where another gray-haired temple patron whispered my "new name" in my ear. Although I'll never be told Brian's "new name," before the ceremony is over, he'll be told mine, which he'll need to remember to call me forth in the resurrection.

Even on resurrection morning, there are added perks of being male.

I stepped into a long line of women who marched quietly into a huge mural-covered room, where we all sat down row-by-row on the left side as the men entered in silence on the right. Brigham Young began this custom of separating Mormon congregations by sex back in 1859, and it's never changed. I strained to find Brian in the sea of male faces. "Together forever" wasn't starting out very together.

During the following two-hour "endowment" ceremony, I received signs, symbols, and handshakes that I would need after I die to pass by the angels and live with God. *No one prepared me for any of this.* I made solemn covenants to obey my husband . . . *Uh oh* . . . to avoid loud laughter . . . *Laughter? Are you sure?* . . . to never speak evil of the Lord's anointed . . . *I would never bad-mouth our leaders* . . . to have sex with only my spouse . . . *Well of course!* . . . and to consecrate everything I had, or ever would hope to have, to the Church of Jesus Christ of Latter-day Saints. *So, tithing is just the beginning. No one told me about this, either.*

And here I always thought it was the other guys, like the Catholics, who got into all that ritual.

A jangling phone yanks my thoughts back from Saturday's solemn events to the Monday morning churning around me. As the day continues, the pestering underwear conversation with Patti nags at me, and I wonder how I can make her understand. I know she'll ask about my garments again, and when she does, I hope I can come up with more convincing-sounding answers.

Since I grew up in a home with parents who wore garments, they're my rite of passage into adulthood. I'm honored, living all wrapped-up, cocoon style, in my beliefs, but Patti doesn't understand why I wear the garments, and to tell the truth, Brian struggles with them too. And although I can't know it then, his getting used to wearing temple garments, along with adjusting to the bigger change of wearing a wedding ring, will never really stick.

At the end of the day, I again pause in front of the gurgling fountain and watch the droplets tumble. How is it possible that something that sounds so simple in church on Sunday can feel so darned tangled up at work on Monday?

NINE

KICKING UP YOUR TAIL
1972

S hallow, like a puddle of water, is the best way to describe the premarital
expertise Brian and I have in *The Joy of* (knowing-nothing-about) *Sex.*
Although we have a high old time fumbling things out, we have lots to learn
about all the splashing and sputtering in this new sensual sea called marriage.
Sex is our bright spot in a host of marital problems.

Brian's conversion to the Church hasn't stuck. Although at first we both
accepted callings and attended meetings galore, now he says, "Whatever I do,
it's just not enough." Do I expect too much from my former altar-boy husband?

Whatever the case, we really need to kick those old inhibitions out of our
bedroom—which is just what my Italian husband has in mind when he suggests . . .

You want to do what?

I've never heard of such a thing. *Could I? Should I? Would I?* I hesitate.
Mormon rules guard every aspect of our lives, and although I've heard some
rumors, I have to be sure what activities must be locked outside our bedroom
door. Can I keep my balance in the bedroom without slipping splat off the
Rock of Mormonism?

Since bishops know all the ins and outs of the sexual rules, I make an
appointment. Once I'm sitting across from Bishop Pritchett in his office, my
hands clutch each other under his large desk, which stretches wide between us.
Its gleaming surface dares me to defile its sanctity with talk of such . . . such . . .

intimacy. My question sticks in my throat. Dare I look him in the eye? A smile flickers under his snow-white hair as he waits. And waits.

Finally, I just blurt it out. "Bishop, does God frown on oral sex?"

My face burns hot. *What must he think of me?* He hesitates and then leans forward against his desk as his lined face softens.

"First of all," he says, "it's important to please your husband."

Whew. My hands loosen their grip on each other and relax in my lap.

"But in the meantime," he continues, "you should pray for him to overcome these desires."

Mama mia! Two giant lobster claws *click-click-click* overhead, pitted one against the other, with me smack-dab in the middle. One claw hangs over me hissing, "Do what your man wants—after all, he's the important male," while the other claw chides me, "But it's still sinful—and here's the kicker—while you're at it, it's up to you to get him to not want it. "

Chiseled into the lobster's underbelly is the real problem—accountability. My husband can be pardoned from enjoying the oral adventure—he's the guy. But the sin still sticks to me.

Instead of enjoying the fireworks, I should pray for God to intervene and douse him with cold water. He enjoys, I pray. Either way, I'm still on my knees.

When can *my* waves of passion be whipped into frothy peaks? Between prayers? But if my husband still feels the urge, my prayers have been worthless. Is God even listening to me? Or are my prayers stuck below the popcorn ceiling in our bedroom because I breathe them out by the same bed in which we break the rules?

Hardly the questions that open the floodgates for sheet-smacking, butt-slapping, headboard-cracking orgasms!

TEN

PINK CORAL SHELLS
1968 – 1985

*B*ack in the year Brian and I married, the freckle-faced neighborhood kid who used to bully my brother came home from his mission. His mission president had given him the standard missionary-going-home advice: "Elder, go home, get married, and start your family. Soon."

Gerald promptly proposed to his fresh-out-of-high school girlfriend and set their wedding date. Soon. He told her their best Christmas present would be to have a baby. Very soon.

But for us, *soon* shuffles its feet, and the years roll on. As Brian is fond of pointing out, we keep practicing, but it just doesn't take.

Still, I trust in the promises of God while I successfully hone my denial skills. If we obey God's commands and have a child, I'm sure God will bless us and bring us closer together. I have faith that then, all our problems will be behind us.

Each year, I dread motherless Mother's Day and the bishop's never-failing announcement across the podium, "Will all mothers please stand to be honored." Women stand up all around me, with motherly pride beaming from earring to earring.

Brian no longer attends. I sit alone.

One close friend at church understands my feelings because prayer isn't filling the crib at her house either. She and her husband finally grow tired of waiting and decide to adopt a child, perhaps a girl, blonde like Annette, or a boy, tall like Paul. I'm so excited about the idea, I eagerly persuade Brian, and we also apply to adopt.

One Friday evening after a busy work week, Annette calls with the big news that their crib will soon welcome an adopted baby boy. She invites us to come and celebrate with them. Talk about timing of the damned—just before we head over to their home, our social worker calls to say she is canceling our request because Brian has told her he couldn't adopt "someone else's" baby. My heart clutches inside, but he refuses to discuss it with me. As we join our friends, I fight back my tears and nail my best stupid smile over my heart.

Church doctrine keeps the pain tacked freshly in place. After all, our prophets tell us if God can't send the spirits from heaven to Mormon homes, He will be forced to send them into the homes of the "wicked." Meaning, of course, homes of non-Mormons.

> There are multitudes of pure and holy spirits waiting to take tabernacles, now what is our duty?—To prepare tabernacles for them; to take a course that will not tend to drive those spirits into the families of the wicked, where they will be trained in wickedness, debauchery, and every species of crime. It is the duty of every righteous man and woman to prepare tabernacles for all the spirits they can. (Discourses of Brigham Young, p. 197, quoted by Prophet Ezra Taft Benson in a Fireside for Parents "To the Mothers in Zion," February 22, 1987, http://fc.byu.edu/pages/ee/ w_etb87.htm)

Therefore, each Mormon family must be willing to have all the babies they can, to provide bodies for the spirit children of God, because all the spirits in heaven must be born before Jesus can return to the Earth. That's some pressure.

It also means God keeps track of His fertile females so He can send bountiful baby bouquets to all the gals who make the grade. This means, of course, I don't. After all, a Mormon woman's purpose for existence is to have babies.

I redouble my efforts to please this God in charge of sending Mormon-rated babies. Blessings have promised me God will strengthen our marriage and send children, so what else does He require of me? Why are the heavens fortified against us? Methodists, Catholics, and Baptists are having babies by the hundreds, by the thousands. Even atheists have babies.

Please, God, what more do you want from me?

But the heavens remain silent, and the years move forward as slowly as a sea turtle dragging one scaly foot in front of the other across the sterile sand. Seven, eight, ten years inch by.

Then at long glorious last, after ten years of trying, I'm pregnant. I know this will fix all the problems between Brian and me.

As we hit the cosmic jackpot, our nighttime sky fills with riotous displays of pink fireworks. Our miracle of new life arrives in the form of the most splendiferous baby girl the world has ever known—thick dark hair, ocean-green eyes, and shell-pink nose, fingers, and toes.

She's so magnificent, I almost feel guilty keeping her because I know how many thousands, tens of thousands, even millions of mothers would give anything for such a child. But then I realize, of all those women, only one could be her mom, and nobody, nobody, could love her as much as I do. I'm sure this beautiful child will help us bridge the distressing distance in our marriage.

I'm expecting our first miracle in 1978.

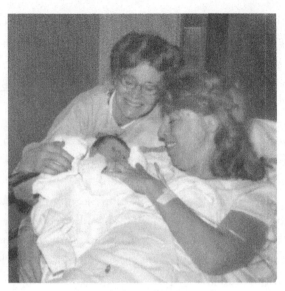

My mom helps welcome our first
gorgeous daughter in 1978.

My mom grabs a ticket for a Greyhound bus and rides twelve hours so she can come and help. God bless mothers.

I'm thrilled to leave the gas company and fulfill my dream of being home to raise our children. Is everything finally coming together? Brian launches a business making marble vanity tops, and I help out part time at his shop, taking our new pride and joy with me. Since he leaves home early and comes home late, at least we can see him for a few hours at his shop.

Brian earns his contractor's license, begins building a home in Cherry Valley for two women on the archery team, and works even later than usual. Going to bed alone gets old. One Saturday night, desperate for him to install some drapery rods, I wait up for him. He finally arrives home after midnight, and he's not happy I'm still up and asking for his help. As he points out, it's the middle of the night. But when else is he home?

Brian loves his daughter, but our distance widens and he rarely spends time with us. Working, working, working. *Working?*

Our bishop, a new convert with a young family, calls me as president of the Primary, the organization for children under twelve. Our ward includes more than a hundred of these young blessings, and one of them is ours. I spend more than twenty hours a week planning, supervising activities, and meeting with my counselors and teachers. Although the Church always insists that moms don't work outside the home, performing such work for them is a seahorse of an entirely different color.

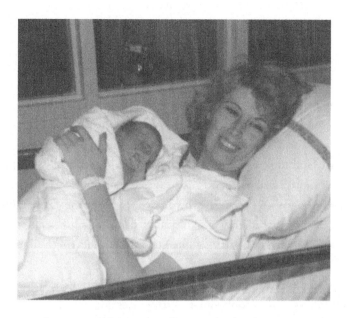

Our second glorious bundle joins the family in 1980.

Always an optimist, I buy a double stroller while praying we can keep the heavens propped open. Yes! In two years, more pink fireworks spray across the evening sky as another gorgeous baby girl joins our family.

I'm thrilled to have my beautiful daughter, and also thrilled my mom is waiting when I get home from the hospital. Again, she takes a bus to come and help, although I need more help than my mom can give. But instead of being brave enough to face our marital problems, I decide to focus on being the best mom I can be to our two wonderful little girls.

Soon after, I find a class called "Creative Experiences for Children" at our local junior college, the same college Brian attended for four years while he shot on the archery team. With a two-year-old and an infant to entertain, I sign up for the class and soon bring other day-care children into our home to divvy up the fun. We make teddy bear bread, paint on easels, and finger-paint with shaving cream, all the while adding a few dollars to the family pot.

Brian wants to build a spec home, finds a lot in Hesperia "up the hill" from San Bernardino, and draws the plans. He pounds two-by-fours into walls, raises them to support rafters, and shingles the roof. About this time, we decide that rather than sell this handsome home, we should be the lucky people to live in it, so we move our family to the high desert, where Joshua trees lift prickly arms in welcome.

After we settle in, I continue doing child care, which grows like Noah's ark, bulging with critters at every door. Brian closes the marble business, tries roofing, works for a tile company, and then opens another shop building custom cabinets. Anything he can get sawdust out of, he loves. But he locates a place for his new shop back "down the hill," which guarantees that his long hours away from home will continue.

A couple of years later, I have more fantastic news, but on a family vacation in Utah, I miscarry. Despair, distress, and depression gnaw at me. I know in my heart God took back His blessing because I haven't measured up.

A few more years pass, and the heavens again split wide open with glorious news of another baby. This pregnancy is the most challenging of the three, not just because of churning morning sickness, but because of the deep fractures in our marriage. Brian still insists, for the umpteenth time, that he is leaving.

I beg him, "Please, please, don't leave us until after the baby is born." I know my role as a Mormon woman is to bear children and trust in God, but how can I survive being pregnant, with two other small children, if he leaves us now?

Amidst his threats of leaving, Brian worries our luck might run out and we'll get a boy. But once again, he gets his wish. Our marital sky may be dark, but the fireworks that again shoot above us light it up with colors that are splendiferously—baby girl pink.

Even our beautiful daughter can't magically mend our marriage, however.

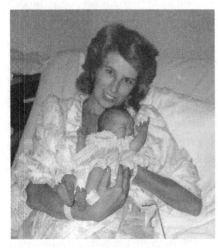

Our third magnificent baby girl arrives in 1985.

The day after her birth, my doctor strides into my hospital room to sign my release papers. A large official-looking man, he scans my chart and readies his pen.

"Please, Doctor Eastman," I plead, embarrassed by my tears as well as my request, "I can't go home today. I need more time."

He lifts his eyes from my chart, pen still poised. "Why?" he asks. "Having some kind of pain?"

"No." I hesitate, not wanting to tell my hell-tale to anyone, especially a stranger. "But my husband is going to leave me as soon as I go home with the baby, and I'm not strong enough to face that yet."

Disbelief covers his face as he asks, "And another day will make a difference?"

"One more day, yes, will help."

Showing his ire, he demands, "Why in the hell did you get pregnant when you're having such marital problems?"

I bite my lip. *How can I explain to a nonbeliever about the promises of God? How can I explain how God granted me this blessing and how according to His almighty will, this child should join our family? How can I explain we were married in the temple, and the purpose of my life hinges on staying in the marriage and raising children in righteousness?*

I can't explain it, but perhaps the fear in my eyes causes him to relent. With a flurry of his pen, he extends my hospital stay for one more day under one condition—that I'll call the number on the card he hands me and make an appointment with a family counselor.

Once I return home, Brian's threat of leaving hangs over us like a menacing gray cloud. I make the promised appointment with the counselor. Brian won't come. He says I put the Church before him and he doesn't think counseling can change anything. Does he have a point? I know if I can only be a better Mormon, God will be pleased and will bless us with a better marriage, so doesn't that mean God and Church *have* to come first?

I drive an hour to San Bernardino to talk to this counselor, but I'm not sure if a non-Mormon can understand a Mormon woman's role. She's a professional woman whose age-lined face exudes experience. I imagine she's heard every tale of marital discord imaginable, and by the worn-down expression in her eyes, I guess most of the stories weren't happy ones.

She suggests I read the book *Women Who Love Too Much*, the title of which leaves me confused. Is it possible to love too much? I confess that after all these years, I feel numb to Brian's continued threats of leaving, and deep inside, part of me doesn't believe he will ever go.

She tries to jolt me back into reality by asking, "And what will you do, if he does leave?" I don't have an answer. Just what is it I could do, anyway, with two small children and an infant to care for? But one person getting marriage counseling can't change the course of two lives, and after a short time, she says unless Brian comes with me, she sees no point in continuing our sessions.

When our newest daughter is a few weeks old, we plan to present her to our ward family. Dad takes a bus from Salt Lake to be a part of this happy occasion, and to stand as part of the priesthood circle where she will be given a name and a blessing. Only priesthood holders can perform this blessing ordinance, which means the father or another male family member if they are worthy, but because Brian rarely attends church, our bishop has to determine if Brian will be allowed to bless his daughter. Not only is my father here to share in the occasion, he's here as my backup.

Hallelujah—Bishop Thaggard bends the rules and allows Brian the opportunity to bless his daughter. Perhaps the bishop hopes this will draw Brian back into the Church.

On that special Sunday, I dress our new daughter in the same white, lacy dress my other daughters had worn. I tie the delicate bonnet my mom had made on her tiny head. When time for her blessing comes, like generations of Mormon women before me, I hand her over to the men. Brian stands in the all-male circle in front of the congregation. Each man puts his left hand on the shoulder of the man on his left, and extends his right hand inside the circle supporting our baby daughter. It's a sacred moment, even from the outside.

Shh, Grandpa and baby are sleeping, 1985.

After the meeting, I take pictures for our family album of the men who stand in the circle. My father, Bishop Thaggard and other male friends give wide smiles as I click the camera, but my husband isn't in the pictures. Right after his "Amen," and long before the meeting ends, he leaves and goes back down the hill. He says he's working, working, working.

But I'm still confident God will bless us with the kind of marriage He has promised me in priesthood blessings if I just read more scriptures! Pray harder! Keep the house cleaner! Keep paying my tithing! Cook better meals! And be the best Mormon wife I can be!

In other words, I know I can navigate through all these rough waters. It just takes a giant dose of denial, masquerading in the white flowing robes of faith.

ELEVEN

FISH STORY
(The One That *Should* Get Away)
1978

A tsunami's heading straight for the shores of Mormonism.

While fireworks would shoot high in the sky of my personal life and we would celebrate the birth of our first child in 1978, another historic landmark event occurred.

On an unsuspecting June morning just four months before the arrival of our first daughter, the big news races through the phone line into my office area at the gas company.

"Did you hear?" my Mormon friend asks breathlessly. "Sorry to call you at work, but this news can't wait."

"Elaine, are you okay?"

"Yes, but you're not going to believe this." Her enthusiasm spills out over my receiver. "Prophet Kimball just announced—blacks can now hold the priesthood!"

"What? But . . . but . . . blacks can *never* hold the priesthood." I say, slapping off my Selectric II typewriter. "Maybe in the next life," I say half to myself, "but not now. It's impossible."

"I'm shocked, too. You know Beverly from Sunday school?"

"Of course." Beverly and her husband are the only interracial couple I've ever known.

"I called her," my friend blusters on, "and told her the news. But she thought I was just playing a cruel joke and hung up on me."

"My gosh! What did you do?" I ask, standing up but keeping my voice low.

"I called her back to tell her it's true. I'm excited for them. Now they can go to the temple and be married for time and all eternity. She was so happy, she cried. Hey, there's more, but you're at work. I'll call you tonight."

Can this news be real?

But real it is, and this change of doctrine will affect the size of the Mormons' so-called fastest-growing flock, because some members will leave now that the flock includes sheep that are black.

Just then, the office door in front of me bursts open as my stocky Mormon boss heads out for lunch, pulling on his sports jacket as he strides past my desk. But when I tell him my "black is in" news, he stops in his tracks. Thunderstruck, he shoos me into his office where we can talk Mormon one-on-one. We both know the reference from *Mormon Doctrine*, which most Mormons consider right up there with scriptures:

> Negroes in this life are denied the priesthood; under no circumstances can they hold this delegation of authority from the Almighty. ... The negroes [sic] are not equal with other races where the receipt of certain spiritual blessings are concerned, particularly the priesthood and the temple blessings that flow therefrom, but this inequality is not of man's origin. It is the Lord's doing, is based on his eternal laws of justice, and grows out of the lack of spiritual valiance of those concerned in their first estate. (Bruce R. McConkie, Mormon Apostle, "Negroes," *Mormon Doctrine*, 2nd edition, pp. 527-528)

What stuns us most of all is that with no more warning than the weatherman canceling a forecast of rain, a basic Mormon doctrine known as the curse has been tossed overboard.

This story of the curse, well known to Church members, explains the beginning of the black race. We've been taught that each spirit is born as a spirit child of God the Father and one of His wives in heaven. While we lived in this pre-Earth state, a war broke out among all the spirit children of God, where some of us sided with Jesus, some sided with his brother Satan, and some didn't choose sides at all. Those non-valiant souls who didn't choose and sat on the fence of indecision got more than splinters in their backsides—God cursed them with a black skin.

These non-decisive souls are then born through the lineage of Cain, of Cain and Abel fame, whom God cursed with a black skin, or "mark," as the Bible says. Joseph Smith expanded those Biblical verses in his Book of Abraham, to explain "that race which preserved the curse in the land" after the flood.

Questions bob around us like corks in a restless sea. Will previous prejudiced statements against blacks be recanted? Does this mean the blacks *were* righteous in the heavenly realms before birth, or has God finally forgiven them for their fence-sitting? And biggest of all, were the prophets wrong, or has God changed His Almighty mind?

The myriad questions the tsunami washes up lie strewn over the sands of time, waiting for the dignity of answers. "Follow the current brethren" will be the only explanation the men in suits will send shooting down the doctrinal pike for more than thirty years.

Thirty-four years later, with the presidential election of 2012 in full swing and Mormonism in the spotlight, we will hear "The origins of priesthood availability are not entirely clear," and that "Previous personal statements do not represent Church doctrine." No mention will be made that many of these "previous personal statements" were made by prophets of God, the same prophets whom, after they speak, "the thinking is done."

On December 10, 2013, a full thirty-five years after the 1978 revelation, and five days after the death of Nelson Mandela, a statement issued on the Church website lds.org will make the Church's stance official: *Denying the priesthood to blacks had really never been Church doctrine.*

Instead, blocking the blacks from the priesthood, from the temple, from the glory of Mormon's highest heaven, had been a carryover from the thinking of the times. A mere misunderstanding. And now, the misguided boat had been righted.

As long overdue as this enlightened statement attempting to distance the Church from racism will be, however, it will be published only on the Church website without any publicity or fanfare.

Not only doesn't the Prophet sign it, he doesn't mention it, allude to it, or speak about it. Neither will it be publicly announced at the semiannual general conference, at any stake conferences, nor at any ward meetings. These omissions guarantee that Mormons sitting in Sunday school will not know anything about it. Perhaps the biggest omission of all, however, is that the statement will not include any apology to African Americans for the racial statements of past decades.

Even the good news in 1978 means only a partial victory—the priesthood that opens its doors to black males is still a boy's club. Half the population of the planet, the female half, is still not allowed to hold the priesthood. Maybe women mucked up in that heavenly war, too, although I've never heard it explained this particular way. Perhaps Mother Eve is once again the culprit. Or, maybe the truth is as simple as Mary Daly said: "If God is male, then male is God."

Long after my boss makes it out the door for lunch, I pat my growing belly and say softly, "Who would have guessed it, little one? You'll grow up in a completely different Mormon world than your mother did. The Church you'll know will allow black men to pass the sacrament, baptize new members, and even attend the temple."

Could this new day signal a wave of change for women too? But then I wonder, how realistic is it for Mormon women wanting equality to stand passively by, waiting for permission from Mormon men?

Instead, maybe we should take a lesson from the spirited ladies with the sensual scales and sinuous tails and realize that equality for women will come to us only when we have the courage to do the outlandish, the outrageous, and—create it for ourselves.

TWELVE

CHILLING
1984

"*A*re you crying?" my mom asks. Her voice sounds weary, as if it has lost energy every mile it has traveled over the long phone wires extending from her phone in Utah to mine in California.

"No," I whisper, sitting down on the family room floor next to my daughters, three and five, who are busy stacking a tower of colored blocks.

Is my answer hurtful? Although I answered truthfully, as she's always taught me, is this one of those times I should have squeezed out a lie? Though there aren't tears on my cheeks, my heart beats through mud and my breath pushes in and out through thick sand. Is this the way my whole body cries when I know I'm going to lose my mother?

She's only sixty-four and has been fighting this damnable cancer for almost a year. She's fought it with radiation from the doctors and blessings from the priesthood, but her weak voice tells me she's losing the battle.

My hand touches my belly, which holds a third grandchild she'll never see. Never read stories to. Never dance with.

Her voice picks up a little energy as she says, "I had Lisa make a sign. Your sister is such an artist."

Thank goodness Lisa lives close by, but I'm surprised at Mom's change of topic. "A sign? What kind of sign?"

"One that says, 'Welcome Home Jason.'"

I cringe inside. *Oh please, Mom, don't do this.*

Although we pray for my brother every morning and every night, we don't talk about him much anymore, especially around Mom. Not since voices of mental illness whispered their way into his mind during his mission, and he finally took off after he graduated from BYU.

Squeals of laughter jar me back to the present as the tower of plastic blocks first wobbles, then tumbles to the floor. The heap lies in disarray all around us. My girls giggle at the chaos, shove the toys to the side as they quickly lose interest, and run outside to play. I'm left alone with my mom and my thoughts.

All this time, over seven years now, a question has gnawed at my insides and tormented my thoughts. Like my brother, like all Mormons, I've been raised to seek inspiration from God.

Moses found a burning bush, and God spoke to him. Joseph Smith prayed in a grove of trees, and God appeared to him. Mormons revere Joseph, our first prophet, who restored God's True Church to the earth, and revere his startling example of receiving personal revelation.

But here comes the tricky part. How do you tell the difference between the whisperings of the spirit and the voice of schizophrenia? If you hear a voice inside your head, does that mean God's richest blessings are falling upon you? Or does it mean the demon of psychosis should be wrestled to the ground with pills? I doubt our family will ever know this answer. The only thing I know for sure is that if I ever get the chance, I'll ask God.

"It's on the piano," Mom says, breaking into my thoughts.

"Why, Mom, why the sign? And why on the piano?" I finger a blue block.

"If he walks by the house and looks through the front window, he'll see it."

My hand freezes in place as I try to reason with her. "Why would he walk by? How would he see the sign from the street, anyway? The house is too far back, and there are trees in the yard."

"God could make him come by and help him read the sign in the window, touch his heart so he'll forgive us, especially forgive me, for having him committed." Her voice trails off at the horror of her memory. "And he'll come home."

I share her desperate concern. We all do. We ache for him, hope he's safe somewhere, and taking his meds. But we've heard nothing from him since he took off seven years ago.

She continues, "They shouldn't have released him from the mental hospital so soon. Your dad and I shouldn't have gone to the temple that day. We shouldn't have left the house. We should have been here, right here, and maybe it would have changed things. Maybe he wouldn't have left. I don't understand. Why did he leave?"

"I don't know, Mom," I whisper. None of us knows. That's the worst pain of it, the not knowing.

"I . . . I want to see my son," she stammers.

Even in Mom's weakened state, I understand how she gave Lisa no choice but to make the sign and place it prominently on the top of the piano. Mom always gets her way. I can picture it hovering over the old ivory keys, across from the big plate-glass window that separates the light in the house from the darkness covering the street. The darkness that somehow holds my brother.

The sign sits on the piano, week after week, projecting guilt and loss and abandonment edged with the faintest glimmer of Mom's hope. It's there still when she dies in the next room. It's there when I come back home to attend her funeral. It's still there that afternoon when a messenger brings a proclamation from the mayor of South Salt Lake City, a family friend, saying the flag will be lowered to half-mast that day to commemorate her. We're moved at the honor.

An unexpected smile comes over my dad's face when he takes the notice. He reads it again and again, tracing the words with his fingers. When he's satisfied it's real, he moves with hesitant steps to the piano, removes the welcome sign, and puts the mayor's proclamation in its place.

He knows Jason isn't coming back.

And neither is Mom.

My father throws himself into composing a memory book of Mom's life called *Our Flora Book* to help stave off his loneliness. He's always been happiest behind his typewriter. When he finishes a year and a half later, the binder bulges with pictures, stories, poetry, certificates, copies of her paintings, memories gathered from family and friends, and yes, even a picture or two of a mermaid with long red hair.

Nearly forty-two years before, Mom donned her white wedding dress, Dad donned his white suit, and hand in hand, they entered the Salt Lake Temple. Inside, in a special sealing room set aside for this purpose, they knelt across a white altar from each other and an officiator of the "one true Church" married them for time and all eternity. He also bestowed upon them ". . . the blessings of kingdoms, thrones, principalities, powers, dominions and exaltations, with all the blessings of Abraham, Isaac and Jacob . . . "

These temple vows sustain his belief that he will again hold Mom's hand as part of an eternal couple, but this assurance also complicates things. If he remarries in the temple as the Church instructs, he will be forever sealed to both women when he dies. On resurrection morning, he'll take both of their hands and the three of them will walk past the trumpeted angels and over the threshold of heaven. He takes this doctrine seriously.

As he thinks it through, he wonders how heavenly things would be if the wives don't like each other. My dad is the only man I've ever known who considers how complicated the afterlife might be if his wives bicker. The logical solution is—and my father is always very logical—to make sure his second wife gets along with the first one. Isn't it just a good idea to keep heavenly problems to a minimum?

After dancing with Mom only for so many years, Dad pushes himself to attend Church singles' dances where he meets new friends. Within a few years, he meets Ettie, a divorcée with several ex-husbands in her marital closet, and a new convert to the Church. She moved from back east to live in Utah "with the saints." Dad sees an opportunity to teach her gospel truths. As their courtship continues, he loves sharing Mom's memory book so Ettie can get to know his late wife.

Later, he pops the big question. "Do you love Flora?" he asks. When she says yes, he pops the next question. "Will you marry me?" When she again says yes, they don't their white temple clothes, enter the Salt Lake Temple, and marry for time and all eternity.

As in most religious doctrines, this sealing-forever concept is weighted with advantages for the male. The man can be sealed to two women, to three women, to many women (too many women!), but a woman can be sealed to only one man.

Dad and Ettie begin their new journey together as husband and wife. And like the rest of our family, their daily prayers always include Jason.

Eight years later on one of our vacation trips to Utah, my girls and I walk with Dad and Ettie on Temple Square, continuing our long-held family tradition. My girls laugh as he jokes about his bald head being cold. He tells me with pride, "I don't take a single prescription." He shuffles a bit as he walks now, but his sturdy cane steadies him. Not bad for seventy-eight.

Those bushy eyebrows of his now adorn a character of an old man, one who always makes me smile. The dad I used to know was always content to be in the background, not wanting the spotlight, but as he's aged, he's come out of his shell. Now he doesn't take life so seriously. He pokes fun at himself, and he chuckles more.

He also starts exploring ideas, although I'm shocked when he says, "If the Church knew what I really believe, they'd excommunicate me." My dad? Where have his years of study led him? But he keeps his radical ideas—if indeed they are radical—to himself. Maybe in this late stage of life, children grown, house paid off, he figures it's okay to enjoy himself, at least for as long as the gods that be have allotted him and his bald head to be.

During our visit, Dad invites me and my daughters, Lisa with her three children, and Ettie to watch a live performance of *Fiddler on the Roof* while we sprawl on the grass in Murray Park. Two days later, after making plans for our next visit home, I drive us back to California with the lyrics of "If I Were a Rich Man" playing in our heads.

A week later, my daughter runs into my bedroom and hands me the phone after breaking our major don't-wake-Mom-under-any-circumstances rule. It's way too early on Sunday morning.

"He's dead!" a voice shouts in my ear.

"What? Who's this?"

"Lisa! I had to call you!"

"Who's dead? Van?"

"Last night he had stomach pains . . ."

Poor Lisa. Van's only in his forties. What could have happened to her husband?

"Lisa, I'm so sorry, what happened?" *What will she do? And with three kids!*

" . . . and Ettie took him to the hospital . . ."

"What? Ettie took him?"

"Of course Ettie. Why not Ettie?"

"Van?"

"No! Dad! Dad's dead!"

I jerk straight up in bed. My mouth is dry and my throat locked shut. Dad's gone. As sudden as that. His pancreas lost out to a gallstone. We never finished our talks on gospel topics. He never answered all my questions. My daughters won't get to really know their grandpa. He never saw his son again. It's all so desperately unfair.

Within another week, we are again standing by a damn coffin and saying good-bye. At least because of their temple marriage, Mom and Dad are together in heaven—at least that—despite Ettie, who tears up his will and absconds with most of our inheritance.

The cold hard facts are—will or not, willing or not—Ettie remains sealed to my dad, which means she belongs to him for eternity and will not be able to remarry in the temple. If she wants to go to the temple and marry another Mormon man for eternity, well, she's simply sunk.

This practice of marrying more than one spouse is called polygamy, which Joseph Smith notoriously instituted into the Church in 1833 in Ohio, with his marriage to sixteen-year-old Fanny Alger—shortly after they were caught together in a haystack—and unknown to his wife Emma. Although illegal, Joseph proclaimed polygamy as a requirement to be exalted in the highest Mormon heaven. Joseph swore to the skeptical that an angel with a sword appeared before him, threatening to kill him if he didn't embrace polygamy—and embrace it he did. And embraced. And embraced. And embraced.

Emma was taken to task with her own personal admonition from the Lord via her husband, Joseph Smith:

> And I command mine handmaid, Emma Smith, to abide and cleave unto my servant Joseph, and to none else. But if she will not abide this commandment she shall be destroyed, saith the Lord; for I am the Lord thy God, and will destroy her if she abide not in my law. (*Doctrine and Covenants* 132:54)

Such a godly threat would motivate most women to accept polygamy.

The *Doctrine and Covenants* is a compilation of Smith's revelations, which Mormons consider canonized scripture, along with the Book of Mormon and the Bible. Joseph's scriptures outweigh Biblical scriptures, however, because of all the pesky errors included in the Bible. As Joseph Smith himself clarified,

I believe the Bible as it read when it came from the pen of the original writers. Ignorant translators, careless transcribers, and designing and corrupt priests have committed many errors. (*Teachings of the Prophet Joseph Smith,* Joseph Fielding Smith, ed., 1938, p. 32)

Fortunately for Mormons, Joseph Smith didn't make such errors. And Joseph Smith believed in polygamy. Although Joseph first kept this belief secret, when word leaked from his inner circle and it became public, it was one of the reasons neighbors drove the early saints from their homes. They didn't want to live among people who married off their young daughters to old men who already were married.

Polygamy will be restored when the Mormon Jesus returns to Earth.

Polygamy is the way devout Mormons anticipate living in heaven.

Polygamy is the lifestyle the Mormon God lives.

Polygamy is like chilling tainted water squirting out from the history of Mormonism.

The Church tries to escape its polygamous past, as well as news stories about current polygamous groups, by claiming it discontinued polygamy in 1890 when it issued "The Manifesto." This Manifesto allowed Utah to be admitted as a state to the union, but polygamy continued in the new state for decades. Although illegal under the law, it was still practiced under Church laws.

The law of polygamy still stands as a requirement in Mormon canonized scripture. Men, like my dad, are still sealed to more than one woman. Mormons still anticipate living polygamy in heaven—except in heaven, it will be like in the good old days of Mormonism.

The Church's claim that it's abandoned polygamy is like sticking a tiny finger into a hole in a dam. No denial can plug a leak against the tide of truth. The swirling complicated problems just keep oozing out and dribbling on through.

THIRTEEN

WARNINGS OF TURBULENCE
1984

*A*ccording to my well-charted plan, my life should glide through placid waters like a sailboat pushed along by blissful breezes through the adventurous waves of life.

While I wait for this fantasy to come true, however, I have found my life looks suspiciously more like a rowboat without the luxury of sails to harness the power of the wind. Luckily for me, my rowboat is equipped with two sturdy oars—faith and prayer.

Mighty blessings lie in store, I know, but before I can receive God's promises of a happy marriage, I must qualify. I must be a good enough wife, a good enough mother, a good enough Mormon. God will come through.

The word *divorce* never blips across my radar screen. After all, Brian and I have been sealed in the Los Angeles Temple for eternity. You don't thrust aside a temple marriage. Marriage means success; divorce means failure. White. Black. I know my role.

I knew my role back when Brian returned from Viet Nam and went to a counselor who diagnosed his continuing depression as caused by him not dating enough before getting married. The non-Mormon counselor suggested the *obvious* solution—Brian should date. Imagine paying sixty dollars an hour to a *marriage counselor* to tell my husband to date other women!

I was so shocked, I made an appointment with the therapist so I could hear those words come out of his mouth for myself. He repeated his dating-around advice and with a swish of his short-fingered hand dismissed my concern about Brian's service in Vietnam being a part of his depression or problems in our marriage.

Why not? After all, what happens inside a boy who goes off to war to be hardened to fight and kill for his country? What happens again when he returns home? Is peace magically returned to his heart when his boots step back onto home soil? Does the love he left with for family or friends remain uncharred by the fires of war he endured, or do those fires still rage deep inside, never to be quenched?

They certainly won't be quenched by dating other women.

But I wasn't the therapist, only the wife who lived with the soldier who came back from Vietnam a changed man. I had to push these questions aside and just get through each day.

Although I knew I had promised in the temple to be obedient to my husband, the humiliation still stung as he spent time with Katie, an outdoorsy gal from the archery team. He insisted they were just friends. Friends who went out to dinner—while I stayed home, alone.

My role meant obeying my husband, accepting a marriage fraught with the constant threat of his leaving. But how long would it be until I came home from work one day to find him gone and his side of the closet empty?

Then, as now, I knew my role.

I continue to cling tightly to my oars of faith and prayer to improve our marriage. In other words—I must *row harder!* I still have confidence in our marriage and in our future together because I'm living gospel principles, and because of our daughters. They have always been, and still are, the bright spot in our rocky marriage.

At a kindergarten parent-teacher open house, I note with pride the picture our oldest daughter has drawn of Humpty Dumpty perched on his famous brick wall. I compare her picture with all her classmates' pictures and discover she alone has captured the concept of staggered bricks. We obviously have an artistic genius on our hands! But Brian isn't here with us, so I can only share the big news with him later, when I call his shop after the girls are asleep.

Bishop Ulrich calls me to write and direct a road show, a twelve-minute play using as many youth and adults in the ward as possible, like the road shows I was part of years ago. But instead of a theme like the one from my teen years, "It's a Gentleman's World That We Live In," I write a script called, "How Cupid Came to Be," which includes parts for children. This also means my daughters can be part of the production and attend rehearsals with me. But Daddy always works.

Row harder!

Mommy-and-me swimming lessons splash through our summers. Our autumns burst with the vivid colors of bright orange dresses, overlaid with yellow ruffled pinafores, which my girls wear to perform in a group called Sunshine Generation. As a part of this children's group, they sing and dance their enthusiastic routines at local churches, nursing homes, and the county fair. We also memorize times tables, master spelling words, and create blue-ribbon science fair projects.

After school, I read them stories. Before bedtime, I read them scriptures. Monday evenings, we have Family Home Evenings, the Church program that designates Monday evenings as family night. But we say family prayers without Dad, and I put the girls to bed by myself.

Row harder!

Sundays, I take the girls to church by myself. One week while I'm wrestling with a new baby and her two older sisters, my three-year-old climbs onto my lap and keeps putting her hands all over my face. After repeatedly brushing her hands away, I ask impatiently, "Why do you keep sticking your hands on my face?"

She coos back, touching my heart forever, "Because I love your face, Mommy."

If only her Daddy were here to share in the moment.

Row harder!

I up my creative spice. Not the kitchen kind, mind you, the cellophane kind. After hearing a fun husband-pleasing idea, I make the plan to wrap my naked self in it and stand inside the front door as a surprise for Brian's late homecoming. Since his shop is forty-five minutes away and his late arrival time completely unpredictable, I call him several times to find out when he'll leave so I can choreograph my wrapping. I don't want to stand here wearing only goose bumps and Saran Wrap for hours, although I know that checking up on him never goes well, no matter the reason. And it doesn't. As he comes through the door, I immediately jump to explain why I called, hoping to lessen his obvious irritation at my calls and to get him to appreciate my see-through attire. Which it does.

I bone up on oral techniques.

I take him out to dinner and slide a key across the table to a motel room I rented that afternoon with my friend Barbara's help. We had a blast hanging sexy lingerie from the chandelier and throwing more across the bed. Fun! No special garments in sight. I tell Brian the girls are spending the night at

Barbara's house. She encouraged me to enjoy this special time she's helped me create. "Don't pick the girls up until noon," she tells me. "Play around. Go out to breakfast."

But the next morning, Brian insists we get up early, pick the girls up early, so he can get back to work early. I stand on Barbara's front step ringing the bell, embarrassed to be so early, and hoping their family is up.

Nothing seems to close the distance between us.

Row harder! And smile.

The toughest rowing challenge of my life, however, looms ahead.

One night, hours after I have tucked the girls in bed, Brian comes home and tells me to follow him into the garage.

"The garage?" I ask.

"Come with me," he insists.

He doesn't want me to wake the girls. He knows I'll scream.

He's having an affair, and he's moving out.

I hold the blinding pain within. I don't tell the girls Daddy left. No reason to. They see him so rarely, they don't even notice he doesn't live with us anymore. I can't go to Bishop Thaggard for counsel, because I'd have to reveal Brian's transgression. That wouldn't be right, would it? No. I won't betray my husband. I keep the hell storm all inside.

Month after month after month thrashes by. The moon and stars continue their treks across the nighttime skies, pretending to the universe, just like me, that nothing has changed.

Then, like a storm blowing up on shore, Brian insists he has ended the affair and wants us to fix things. Can we? I don't know. He confesses his affair to Bishop Thaggard.

Soon afterward, I also make an appointment with our bishop, feeling in desperate need of counsel and guidance. My friend Becky watches the girls while I drive to the church on a Sunday evening to meet with him, a handsome man around forty, some years younger than I. He greets me inside his office and motions me to sit down before taking a seat behind his desk. I spill it all—Brian's moving out, his affair, my fears for the future.

When I finish, he leans back in his chair for a moment, as if considering. After a pause, he offers his shepherding advice: "It's kind of like a tennis ball that's painted green on one side and yellow on the other side."

I don't move. *What?*

He continues, "It all depends on which side you're on, what color the tennis ball is."

My mouth falls open, but no words come out as I try to get my brain cells to line up. *What does divorce have to do with tennis balls of whatever color? Besides, we're not talking about a tennis ball; we're talking about adultery. Members get excommunicated for adultery—don't they?—especially with the "next to murder" doctrine.*

"But, won't there be a Church court?" I stammer.

"I don't know if there will or not. It would all depend."

Depend? On what?

"But if there *is* a Church court . . ."

If?

". . . you should know that you can't be there, and you won't be told the court's decision."

"Why won't I be told?"

"If your husband wants to tell you what happens, then that's up to him. But otherwise, you won't know. It's strictly between Brian and the Church, not you."

My brain cells huddle in confused clusters as I stare at my bishop. I'll find no help here. After I leave his office, I walk to the car alone through the dark parking lot, my stomach clenching inside.

Row.

Row.

Row.

FOURTEEN

RAGING WATERS
1987

*T*he axis of my world is wobbling. I've got to get out of here. Away. Anywhere. Anyplace else. Instead, I smile. Brian has come to spend time with the girls, and I must pretend I'm fine with this. But my smile is crushing me. *Keep up appearances. Be calm. For their sakes.* But I can't do it for another minute, and Brian will stay for several hours. Our pretend family will have to pretend without me this Sunday night.

"I have to leave," I say, grabbing my car keys and rushing out the front door. I back the car out of the driveway onto the road. I know I don't want to be here, but where am I going? Maybe the mall, where I can melt in with the anonymous faces of strangers.

The road blurs. Signposts seem to weave around. Street lights fade in and out. Where am I? The haze surrounding me clears, and I find myself driving past the church. Automatically, I pull into the crowded parking lot and my Datsun wagon shivers to a stop. But how did I end up here?

The dark parking lot jogs the memory of my visit with Bishop Thaggard just weeks ago. If I walk into the church tonight, will I again leave with a clenched stomach?

I enter the empty lobby. Within seconds, the double chapel doors burst open and an army of dark suits and white shirts appear. Must be a priesthood meeting ending. The first shirt and tie through the door is a friendly familiar face, Brother Dave Sterling, one of Bishop Thaggard's counselors.

He takes one look at me and asks, "Do you need help?"

I nod.

"Stay here for just a minute," he says, putting a supportive hand on my shoulder. "I'll be right back."

Later, I'd learn that because he wasn't the bishop, who was out of town, he'd needed to ask special permission for the two of us to talk in private.

Brother Sterling finds an empty classroom and pulls out two chairs, and I sob out my story.

He throws a lifeline of hope and caring into the raging sea that's my life. He listens, cares, sympathizes. Yes, of course there will be a court. No, this has nothing to do with tennis balls. And, I should get an AIDS test. I haven't even considered the possibility of contracting anything, although I naively believe God would protect me from such an injustice.

Hours later, as we're walking out, the church building feels encased in silence. His caring words have turned the blasting sea within me into manageable waves. I feel that just perhaps, my life is worth the battle after all. I can face going home now.

As we approach the almost empty parking lot together, he says, "I know how difficult life can be. I've been reinstated in the Church myself."

Really?

"And for the same thing."

My gosh. It couldn't be. Not a bishop's counselor.

"Well," he adds almost as an afterthought, "it wasn't about another woman."

But if it weren't another woman, it couldn't be the same thing.

If I were thinking straight, maybe I'd realize what he's saying. And if my crystal ball were working, I might even be able to see that in the not-too-distant-future he would have his membership yanked—not for *being with* another man, but for being *attracted to* men. And if that gazing ball would clear enough for me to see years yet further down the road, once he owned who he really was, I'd see that he'd find what he had searched for all his life—peace and happiness. But tonight, there's no crystal ball for either one of us.

Tonight, I'm just grateful Bishop Thaggard is far away, and instead, Dave Sterling, the best Mormon man I know, was the first to come through the chapel doors and offer me the shepherding help I so desperately needed.

Within a month, and five days before our baby's second birthday, Stake President Jarrett (Church official above Bishop Thaggard) summons Brian to a court presided over by fifteen high priests. If Brian were a woman, it would have been less complicated, since a court for a woman requires only three members of the bishopric and a clerk. Although Bishop Thaggard told me I couldn't attend, Brian tells me of the verdict that the fifteen men pronounce—excommunication.

Now he is no longer a Mormon. Our temple sealing is invalid. We are no longer a forever family.

But Brian moves back in and suggests counseling. With a toddler and two older daughters six and eight, I'm desperate to make it work. Can this be the lifesaver for us? We can try.

We drive an hour and a half to Redlands to see a Mormon counselor, a short man with a limp from a bout with polio as a child. He says we are a first in his career, a couple with big marital problems but who keep their libido going strong in the bedroom. Sex is our glue, but even sex isn't superglue.

Brian tells him, "If it weren't for the Church, we'd have a good marriage." What? Had we lived on separate planets all these years? I've always been a devout Mormon through and through, from the beginning of our marriage. Doesn't he understand what the Church means to me? How can he expect me to put him, or anyone, before the Church?

"If you really want to work through these things and save your marriage, Brian," the counselor insists, "you must actually spend time at home. How often will you commit to come home in time to eat dinner with your family?"

For Brian, being home by dinnertime would be a huge concession.

"Sundays," he says, offering his compromise. "I'll come home in time to eat dinner with my family on Sundays."

We enjoy dinner with Daddy for three Sundays, but by the next week, there are again only four of us around the dining room table.

Row harder!

But two must row together to make progress.

On Brian's forty-third birthday in mid-November, we all head to Sears for a family milestone—a family portrait that includes *him*. Most of the pictures in our family album show just the girls and me. When I pick up the finished pictures, I'm thrilled. Our daughters' beautiful little faces grin wide for the camera. Our two older girls are radiant in matching red sweaters, and our littlest, now four, grins mischievously above a teal turtleneck the same shade as my dress.

I even like the picture of me. I've never been overly confident about my looks, especially considering my appearance when I roll out of the bed in the morning, but I work at it. One advantage of being a skinny kid is turning into a slender adult. Sometimes it all comes together, and in this picture, I can say it, I look pretty. I'm inclining my head slightly toward Brian, his dark hair contrasting nicely with my strawberry blonde hair. His expression is a bit more hesitant than my bright smile, but he's handsome in the dark burgundy sweater I gave him as a birthday present. The picture doesn't record, however, that he's left the tags on it and that before we leave the mall, he returns it for a refund.

For me, the picture snaps a happy moment in time. Things are better, aren't they? Looking at this picture, all I want to see is a loving family. But would a stranger's eye linger a moment on Brian's slightly guarded look? Maybe a stranger's would, but I'm so used to the chill, I'm oblivious to what's really going on.

Row, row, row!

Too late. The same day I bring the girls home from the Victorville Christmas parade, Brian upends our lives by telling me he's moving out. Can't we still make this work?

If I only row harder!

Unbeknown to me, however, the current I'm rowing against is another affair.

Things go to hell and back, month after month. And one year strains into two.

Then, when our youngest is six, the year we would have reached our twenty-fifth wedding anniversary, Brian files for divorce. The pain of severance is searing. No more pretending. Now I must face being left alone and on my own. But I'm not really by myself, for along with being alone comes the responsibility of three young children to care for, to support, and, thank God, to love.

Life forever changes. The day may come when I can actually say my husband's leaving for good is for the best, but that day is far, far away.

FIFTEEN

WINGS OVER THE SEA
1992

*A*s the months go by, I cling to my faith as waves of a life-shattering divorce storm over me. *Please, please, God, help me through this.*

I know since I'm no longer married, I can't be with my family in the highest Mormon kingdom, but right now, I don't have the energy to worry about these kinds of heavenly problems. Earthly priorities take all my time. Priorities like refinancing the house to give Brian half. Paying the bills. Dealing with the stark abandonment I feel, especially every other weekend when he drives off with my three daughters, *my babies,* and his new girlfriend. I stand alone in the middle of the living room. And scream.

I pray hard, create extra projects in the yard, and go to church dances on Saturday nights. One of my favorite scriptures becomes Psalm 139:9:

> If I take the wings of the morning,
> and dwell in the uttermost parts of the sea;
> Even there shall thy hand lead me,
> and thy right hand shall hold me.

Thoughts of soft wings, a bright morning, and a wet sea swirl around in my head. A melody forms and takes flight, first as a solo, then as a majestic piano arrangement. Oh, how I wish I had the know-how to create such music. Then one Tuesday morning, the mailman drops a shiny catalog into my mailbox from the local community college located just eight minutes from my home. Inside its covers, I find courses offered in music theory.

Aha—sign me up.

I soon discover that arranging music is more complicated than piling notes on top of each other. Semester after semester, I study the patterns, structures, and techniques of composition so I can set my favorite scriptures to music.

In my theory classes, I meet talented musicians from other churches. Although I have played the piano and organ at church for most of my life, all of my service, like most other Mormon musicians, has been voluntary. My background, although heavy on experience, has been light on expertise. I soon discover my classmates' secret. Their churches *pay* them to provide the music—*it's their job*.

Getting paid for church service goes against every drop of my Mormon beliefs. Each month when I attend the temple, during the two-hour endowment ceremony film, the actor portraying Apostle Peter preaches that a paid ministry is of the devil, and a lay ministry is a sign of the Lord's True Church. Yet my classmates show me alarming proof of an upside to their "evil" ways of earning a living—they become quality musicians. Instead of music existing as their hobby on either side of a nine-to-five commitment, these artists can jam their whole day with harmony.

But my days are stuffed full supporting my family. Now that I'm divorced, I've increased the number of children who come to my day care, just as I expanded the playground equipment, bumped up the activities, and upped the hours my assistant, "Magic Lisa," comes in to help. At my house, music arranges itself around all sides of kids.

Music also helps keep me and my daughters busy. I read an ad in the paper of a teacher who created a new method for teaching piano, and I sign up my oldest daughter. Within months of lessons, her fingers are flying all over the keyboard. My two younger daughters play at the violin, at least long enough for me to finish making payments on the instrument. I also take guitar lessons and attempt to entertain my daughter's first-grade class.

My daughters go with their dad every other weekend, often to exciting places such as Disneyland, Knott's Berry Farm, or the beach. How ironic—after our divorce, Brian spends time with his girls.

But on those every-other weekends, for me the music stops. I try to outrun my discouraged thoughts by keeping busy. I keep attending church dances, plant rose bushes and honeysuckle vines, and arrange music to my favorite scriptures. A few of my favorites include "Children Are an Heritage of the Lord" (Psalm 127:3), "The Day That the Lord Should Be Born" (Book of Mormon, III Nephi 1:13, 19-21), and "He Is Risen" (Matt 28:1-6).

My biggest musical success comes by having my music scores used for the theme of several singles' conferences.

I continue my music classes and that spring, I get a call from the music director for our stake. She's a tall, no-nonsense kind of woman with wisps of dark hair framing her face. She asks me to accompany a special cantata for the fast-approaching Easter season. I don't know much about her, except that she has a brood of five or six children at home and an accomplished musical background. She doesn't know much about me, either, except she's probably seen me play the organ for sacrament meetings, baptisms, firesides, weddings, and funerals, so she assumes I'm up to this job. But as soon as she shows me the complex organ scores, I know this music far exceeds my abilities.

Still, Mormons don't say no, so I agree. With the first rehearsal a week away and the cantata only a month away, I have precious little time to learn the music, even without attempting those pesky organ pedals. I begin the practicing marathon.

At the first rehearsal, my hands tremble over the keyboard. At our director's downbeat, I begin the introduction, the choir joins in, and I bungle through as best I can. I soon realize the wisdom of playing a one-note melody for each choir's part. Afterward, I rush home and spend two or three hours a day on the piano bench in my family room.

Being true to our "Every Member a Missionary" challenge first issued by Prophet David O. McKay, I invite Luda, a hardworking Russian friend who helps in my day care, to attend the cantata. I also arrange to have a copy of the program translated into Russian for her.

I keep up my daily sessions at the piano and, by Jupiter, after many more hours, on that opening night, I have the notes down smooth as fine sand in a wave-washed bay. When you're a Mormon, especially when you need to keep busy, opportunities just keep pouring in.

As I read again, "If I take the wings of the morning, and dwell in the uttermost parts of the sea, Even there shall thy hand lead me, and thy right hand shall hold me," I feel comfort. Although I certainly could use a strong hand to lead me, even a hand or two to hold me.

But for now, both of the hands seem to be mine, planted firmly on a black-and-white keyboard.

SIXTEEN

WATER WORKS
1993

*A*re those tears dripping down my daughter's face? Why here at church?

Ferociously, she dabs at her puffy eyes and ducks her head as I come near. Always a stubborn soul, she refuses to tell me what's wrong. I can only blot her tears with the pads of my thumbs and clamp my arm around her small shoulders as we zigzag our way through the church parking lot. Although tears are common at our house since Dad moved out, what could have triggered them today at church, after all these months, to start her crying again?

I learn later that her tears, as well as both of her sisters', have followed children's singing time in Primary. The songs tout families are forever themes, or rather families *can* be forever, but Dad doesn't live with us now. He lives with Sandra. No more hopes of being a forever family. Not only are my girls tormented with Dad out of their home, but they are also tormented believing Dad will be out of their heaven. And in another place. Their pain has to spill out somewhere.

The songs the children sing speak of a sweet belief:

> I have a family here on Earth,
> they are so good to me.
> I want to spend my life with them
> through all eternity.
> Families can be together forever . . .

At least I've always considered it a sweet belief. Then I realize that not just my children, but also most of the children in Primary, are doctrinally damned from having their families be together forever.

Divorce is only one reason. Others include a nonmember father, a single mother, a father who smokes, a mother who drinks coffee, or the family who doesn't pay their tithing. These are all heaven-breaking offenses, driving eternal wedges between families in the afterlife. And my daughters aren't the only ones feeling the pressure.

My pressure comes from Max, a guy I meet at a church dance. Although I have a thing for tall men, he's a good dancer, so I'm happy to overlook the fact that he's height challenged. One Sunday, he attends a singles' fireside where the speaker reminds everyone in attendance that to fulfill God's plan, we must be married. He further states that if a man who holds the priesthood proposes to a woman and she turns him down, *for whatever reason*, she jeopardizes her eternal salvation.

Since Max holds the priesthood and has marriage on his mind, he can hardly wait to tell me all about it. When he shares this romantic Mormon logic, I gasp, "Are you trying to blackmail me into marrying you?"

I hope there's a marriage-proposal manual out there somewhere that points out if a man tries to reel in his sweetie with such a line of doctrine-trumps-love, the result can be disastrous. Because it is.

This coveted priesthood is first given to males when they turn twelve years old and are ordained to the office of deacon. When a Mormon boy reaches the age of twelve, fourteen, and sixteen, he is called to the office of, respectively, deacon, teacher, and priest. After that comes the office of elder, high priest, patriarch, seventy, and apostle. And, at the top of the chain, the man who outlives all the apostles named before him, becomes the president or prophet.

I heard of a man who, attempting to prove his membership in order to receive Church welfare, instead of claiming the office of "seventy," said he was an "eighty." Oops—getting that title wrong blew his cover, along with any hope of getting Church assistance.

Priesthood might even be required to save our country. According to an oral prophecy of Joseph Smith, called the White Horse Prophecy, the US Constitution will one day "hang by a thread." This will require a Church elder from Zion, aka Salt Lake City, to ride in on a metaphorical white horse to save the day. I heard my dad talk about the implications of this "prophecy" while I was growing up, but he never could have anticipated how interesting it would make later political races when a Mormon would run for president. Apparently in 2008 at least, Mitt just wasn't the right Mormon elder to save us.

In my life, the concept of priesthood is growing more and more complicated.

A family has to be sealed, a Mormon term meaning connected by priesthood power, to be together in heaven. But I'm divorced and no longer sealed to my husband, so am I still sealed to my parents through my dad's priesthood? Still sealed to my children? Can we still all be unified in Heaven? Or does a priesthood man have to live in my immediate family? It all comes down to one big question—is priesthood a requirement to make a family count?

Apparently.

In fact, when our ward divides in two, it is split so each half will have the same number of priesthood holders, not the same number of members. *Only* priesthood holders are counted. My family of four females doesn't even make the tally. It would be different if one of my three daughters were a twelve-year-old son, as even one twelve-year-old male trumps four females, but because women don't hold the priesthood, we don't count.

Since four females don't count on the Mormon rolls when the Church divides a ward, will we count on the rolls of glory in their heaven? Will that golden list encumber itself with the names of one divorced mother and three daughters who aren't glued together by this priesthood power? Or will that gilded roll contain the names only of those attached with an official priesthood stamp, leaving our names to just slide into the abyss of the unnumbered, uncounted, and un-male?

Perhaps an archangel must announce, "Hold that mother and child still so I can join them together for eternity with this golden thumbtack of her husband's priesthood."

Just what kind of Heaven is this Mormon highest Heaven, which opens its gates only to men who hold the priesthood and only to women who are married to such men? Are rainbows stapled over seascapes by priesthood to keep their colors arched above? And are the clouds glued to the skies with priesthood, too, to keep them from blowing away?

SEVENTEEN

RHYTHM AND BLUES
1993

*I*n one AD (after divorce), I discover a rhythmic freedom of expression called ballroom dancing. I also discover I have a certain flair for this kind of waltz, swing, and fox-trot fun. The dance floor is the place for a good follower to shine, and if ever a gal lived who spent her life learning how to follow, let's just say I'm that gal.

One Saturday night, I waltz with a man who is delighted to dance with a Mormon and is just as determined to show me the cure. Between demonstrating his tango and salsa footwork, my new mustached friend disputes my every Mormon belief. His most outrageous claim is that Joseph Smith, revered founder and first prophet of Mormonism, boasted that he was greater than Jesus Christ. Anti-Mormon propaganda!

To prove his claim false, first thing the next day, I check out his story with an LDS history buff who lives in our ward. He refers me to the Church-published *History of the Church,* written by Joseph Smith. Within its pages, I find the impossible nightmare—Salsa Man has it right. The Church's official history documents that Joseph Smith claimed he had more to boast about than any man who ever lived, even Jesus Christ:

> If they want a beardless boy to whip all the world, I will
> get on the top of the mountain and crow like a rooster. I
> shall always beat them.... I have more to boast of than ever
> any man had. I am the only man that has ever been able

to keep a whole church together since the days of Adam. A large majority of the whole have stood by me. Neither Paul, John, Peter, nor Jesus ever did it. I boast that no man ever did such a work as I. The followers of Jesus ran away from Him, but the Latter-day Saints never ran away from me yet. (*History of the Church of Jesus Christ of Latter-day Saints*, 2nd edition. Vol. 6, 1973, pp. 408-409)

What? My prophet Joseph? My mind flashes back to 1966 when the Beatles proclaimed they were more popular than Jesus, which flamed protests around the world as former fans burned their records. The Beatles' claim was bad enough, but it's far worse for me to discover that years before their fiasco, Prophet Joseph Smith had made the same claim. This fire smells much too close to home.

Later that year, the Church hosts a western dance social. As we all fill the large gymnasium for line dancing, we are greeted by a thin gal with blonde curly hair and red fringy boots who turns up the country music, shouts "five, six, seven, eight," and leads us in a lively grapevine to the right across the gleaming gym floor.

As the two-stepping, old-trucking beat rings out, my own boots long to let loose, boot scoot and boogie, until I remember my old teen idol, Chubby Checker. Way back in my high school days, when his dance sensation "The Twist" spiraled into fame, the Church promptly banned it from all its dances. I got the message loud and clear—hip gyrations mean big trouble.

So before I hit *this* dance floor, I vow to take things nice and easy. Although I admit the urges flow through me to join the beat of the music and let myself go, I hold back.

At the end of the dance as the music fades, a stranger in a dark suit strides across the floor, heading in my direction. He stops up short in front of me, his face so close that his dark-rimmed glasses are inches from my face.

"Sister!" he scolds in a booming voice, his shoulders stiffening with resolve. "*Those* kinds of movements are *not* appropriate in the church house."

Clang. Bars of chauvinism shut tight around me. I stand silent, shrinking into myself, stunned into submission.

Although the western beat starts right back up for the rest of the crowd, for me, the rhythm is gone. Can I get it back?

Later at home, I crank up the volume on my CD player to a fever pitch and slip into a sheer, feather-trimmed peignoir I purchased on a whim and hid in the back of my closet. Time to bring this baby out. I spin, spiral, and swirl through the house, reveling in the rhythmic music as it pulls me in new directions. I immerse myself in the sensual freedom of movement—and not a judgmental eye in sight. Just the beat of the music, the soft delicate fabric, and me, drenched in the pandemonium of the moment, as uninhibited as the thrashing and crashing of the eternal sea against the sandy shore.

This feels more like it.

EIGHTEEN

MOONLIGHT ON MERMAID TAILS
1994

"Where are you, Mom?" my daughter shouts as she wanders out to the backyard.

"I'm back here," I holler, pulling on a weed that has dared sprout among my flowers.

Spotting me, she calls, "I did it!"

She's sixteen, going on all grown up. Her thick dark hair from her dad's side brushes against her olive-skinned shoulders as she hurries across the grass. She looks the most Italian of any of my girls, and *mama mia,* do those genes work for her. I give one big yank on the green intruder, breaking it free from the soil.

"Did what?" I ask, sitting down hard and looking up at her dark eyes glittering with excitement.

"Made my appointment with the patriarch. For this Sunday!"

"Honey, I'm so excited for you."

She sits down by me, plucks a blade of grass, and slides it back and forth between her fingers. Her voice is low when she finally asks, "Do you think I'm ready, Mom?"

I slap dirt off my jeans, wipe my hands on the grass, and slip my arm around her. "Of course I do. Why?"

"Maybe I should wait, fast more, and read more scriptures."

"I know it's a big step, but you're ready," I say, giving her a hug.

I feel nervous too, but I don't tell her. My firstborn daughter has officially come of age, and maybe I'm the one who's not ready. In just five more days, it will happen—she will receive her patriarchal blessing.

For a Mormon, receiving a patriarchal blessing is getting a road map for life, for finding out the blessings God holds especially for you, one to a customer. Like our prophet Thomas S. Monson once explained, "A patriarchal blessing literally contains chapters from your book of eternal possibilities."

I feel a ripple of pride knowing she set it up all herself, went to the required interview with our bishop, and got her Patriarchal Blessing Recommend. She also made the appointment with the stake patriarch, the man ordained to give these blessings. I have grown less and less certain of the power these men hold, but she's excited, she's faithful, so why should I take this away from her? For her sake, I'll hold my doubts in tow.

These blessings are modeled after the blessings Jacob gave his twelve sons in Genesis, except girls get included too. Good news at our house. There are three big things my daughter expects to find out during her special blessing: her past, her present, and, most intriguingly, her future.

The patriarch will reveal her past by declaring her lineage in the house of Israel. It's pretty much a done deal that she comes from the Old Testament tribe of Ephraim, because most Mormons do. But bloodlines can be tricky. Sometimes two people in the same household can have a different lineage proclaimed. It's a complicated lineage thing, but nothing to worry about. The patriarch knows best.

Telling the present is pretty straightforward. I'm sure she'll be told she has "goodly parents," like my blessing says, like most blessings say, patterned after the Mormon prophet Nephi in the opening words of the Book of Mormon: "I, Nephi, being born of goodly parents . . ." Goodly parents means standard Mormon parents.

Now we get to the best part, the truly interesting part, the *future*. What lies ahead for my dark-haired beauty? Marriage, children, missionary service, or church callings generally make this list. And probably a few warnings will be tossed in about avoiding the power of Satan, who always seems fixated on keeping Mormons from the temple. But what possibilities of greater, unknown, and dazzling promises could be ahead for her? We won't know any of this until Sunday.

I explain to her that once she gets her blessing, it will be recorded for posterity. It's that important. One copy will be hers to study throughout her life, and one copy will be kept permanently on file with the Church. Probably even stored inside the huge vaults blasted deep into the solid granite in Little

Cottonwood Canyon, where the Church stores many of the old important journals and papers, so they're all protected even until the second coming.

Sunday takes its ol' sweet time but finally shows up.

She's the first one to pop out of bed and rushes into my bedroom. "Mom, remember to fast with me today!" As if I could forget.

After Sunday school, we have an extra prayer before leaving for Patriarch Henderson's home. When we arrive in our Sunday clothes, I knock briskly on his door.

"Come on in," his wife Arleen says, opening the door wide and ushering us in to the scent of a Sunday dinner bubbling away in the kitchen. If there were a poster for how all Mormon women aspire to look, Arleen's face would be smiling out from the middle of it. Gracious, attractive, and warm. And helpful, as she will record and transcribe the blessing.

Patriarch Henderson shakes our hands, his face laden with soft, experienced wrinkles under graying hair. When the moment comes, he motions my daughter toward a high-backed upholstered chair. He stands behind her and places his hands on her head. She bows her head, preparing for the silent flap of angel wings, and waits for him to pronounce her blessing.

On the drive home, my daughter sobs. Through her tears, she manages to choke out, "Mom, it didn't tell me *anything*."

What can I say? Of course this isn't quite true; her blessing did tell her *something*. It told her she was born of the line of Ephraim, as expected, but that won't have much of an influence on her daily life. It said she was born of goodly parents, special to be born to this Mormon family, and that she could go on a mission if she chose. She was encouraged to be valiant, marry in the temple, and God would bless her. Amen. Pretty well summed it up. All that expected stuff.

But the words spoken over her head held no sparkles or lights of brilliance. Tears tumble down her cheeks all the way home.

I understand her disappointment, although at this point in my life, I admit I didn't expect more, since the magic of Mormonism is wearing thin wherever I look. The blessing she received could have been pronounced on the head of either a boy or a girl. It said nothing just about *her*.

She never reads it again.

Certainly, the Osmond brothers' blessings had been much more interesting. Due to their celebrity status, the *Church News* had run an article about those blessings just the year before. It said back in 1962, when Olive and George Osmond's talented sons were beginning their careers by singing at church and civic groups, a national program had invited the Osmonds to appear on television.

Olive was uncomfortable with the idea. "I would sure feel better about this," she told her husband, "if a couple more of our children were to get their patriarchal blessings." So Alan, twelve, and Wayne, ten, went to receive their blessings. Olive reported, "We came home and started packing our suitcases. We sensed the importance of it, because they were told certain things that were quite thrilling and have come true."

Osmond brother Merrill related specifically, "We would travel all over the world as brothers performing and open the doors for [LDS] missionaries." (*Church News*, week ending August 28, 1993, p. 7). Too bad that patriarch missed one of the brightest stars in the family, a sister named Marie.

But this doesn't seem to be the time to tell my daughter that patriarchal blessings used to be much more interesting, even magical, back in the dawn of early Mormonism. The world around Joseph Smith reveled in such things as gold sought in hillsides, mystical seer stones, and angels revealed in shafts of light.

I also won't tell my daughter how her great-grandmother was promised in her blessing dated May 1, 1903, "thou shalt be one of the chosen number that will be called to go back to the Center Stake of Zion . . . and thou shalt be privelaged [sic] to behold the presence of God upon that land, and of the blessings of that beautiful city that is to be built."

This is Mormon speak for going back to Jackson County, Missouri, to witness the second coming of Jesus Christ.

I certainly won't tell her now that promises of missionary work also used to include converting those on the islands of the sea or in foreign lands to usher in the return of Christ.

It gets even better. The most riveting promises concerning missionary work in the early Church came after a spectacular teaching of Joseph Smith that said people who dressed like Quakers inhabited the moon. Then the ultimate missionary promises began to filter down through patriarchal blessings—

the promise of teaching the gospel to those people on the moon. Now that's the kind of a promise that would set anyone's dorsal fins aflutter.

The references came from diary entries, such as this one.

> Astronomers and philosophers have, from time almost immemorial until very recently, asserted that the moon was uninhabited, that it had no atmosphere, etc. But recent discoveries, through the means of powerful telescopes, have given scientists a doubt or two upon the old theory. Nearly all the great discoveries of men in the last half century have, in one way or another, either directly or indirectly, contributed to prove Joseph Smith to be a Prophet. As far back as 1837, I know that he said the moon was inhabited by men and women the same as this earth, and that they lived to a greater age than we do — that they live generally to near the age of a 1000 years. He described the men as averaging near six feet in height, and dressing quite uniformly in something near the Quaker style. In my patriarchal blessing, given by the father of Joseph the Prophet, in Kirtland, 1837, I was told that I should preach the gospel before I was 21 years of age; that I should preach the gospel to the inhabitants upon the islands of the sea, and — to the inhabitants of the moon, even the planet you can now behold with your eyes. (*The History of Oliver B. Huntington*, p. 10, typed copy, Marriott Library, University of Utah)

Apparently, rocket travel to the moon has some fast catching up to do for Mormon missionaries.

Joseph Smith Sr., the father of Joseph Smith Jr., and first patriarch in the Mormon Church, pronounced blessings full of glitter and gold:

> Thou shalt have access to the treasures hid in the sand to assist thy necessities. An angel of God shall show thee the treasures of the earth that thou mayest have riches to assist thee in gathering many orphan Children to Zion. (From a Patriarchal Blessing of Wilford Woodruff, given by Joseph Smith, Sr., 15 April 1837)

... thou shalt have all power, even to translate thyself and change into a shadow; so that if any shall smite at thee they shall only hit thy shadow, and thou shalt be in another place. (From Patriarchal Blessing of William Harris, given by Joseph Smith Sr., 2 May 1836, Kirtland, Ohio)

... thou shalt have power to translate thyself from one plannet [sic] to annother [sic] — power to go to the moon if thou shalt desire it. (From Patriarchal Blessing of Lorenzo Snow, given by Joseph Smith, Sr., 15 December 1836)

Today, an official Church manual dictates to patriarchs the dos and don'ts of giving patriarchal blessings. I suspect this may explain why present-day blessings have lost their luster. When the rules controlling the communication with the heavens are scribbled down in black and white ledger lines, the magic is sure to suffer.

If the blessings promised by the patriarch don't come about, only two explanations are possible: One, the person simply didn't qualify, so God didn't grant the blessing, or two, God is holding the promised blessing for the next life. Ah, the next life, where we collect all the promised goodies.

As Church leader Richard P. Lindsay explains, "A patriarchal blessing is not having your fortune told. It is a source of guidance as you grow in maturity and spirituality."

Nope, not at all like getting your fortune told. But oh, if you look back to the good old days of early Mormonism, some of them were *just* like that.

NINETEEN

A FINAL WAVE
1996

*C*ertain forces in nature are not meant to collide. Ever. Like colon cancer and my best friend Cindy. But her collision comes clang-clang-
clanging in the night anyway.

Between Cindy and her husband there are ten children, including one
son on a mission in Spain and two teenage boys still at home.

After months of trying different treatments—a diet cooked on a new
kind of stove, a doctor who flew in from the East Coast promising, "I won't let
you die," a specialist at City of Hope, priesthood blessings from her husband
and bishop, massages to relax her body, calm and peaceful meditations—her
cancer cells keep spreading.

I struggle with how to help my friend. By now she spends most of her
time in bed, exhausted and weak. Flowers seem too small a gesture, although
I bring some blossoms from my yard and set them in a colorful vase by her
bed. Other friends clean her house and bring her meals, but I need to do more.
Her body hurts. Can I help relieve her pain? I finally figure it out—I can mas-
sage her back and legs an hour a day.

But when? Motherhood runs around the clock, day care goes crazy all
day long, and church meetings plug up most evenings. That's it. The meetings—they'll have to go. Or rather, I won't. I need to do something far more
important.

The truth is, I have some big-time baggage to atone for. I need to do for
my friend Cindy what I failed to do for my mother. Twelve years earlier, when

doctors diagnosed my mother with cancer, I put off making plans for a final visit with her in Salt Lake. Although my two little girls and I had gone for one visit and planned another trip that chicken pox derailed, we'd needed to visit again while we still could.

Kids and trips always kick up complications. I was pregnant with our third child, and I also had to make arrangements for the day-care children. But a bigger problem hung over me. I had committed to play the piano for our ward's road show, which rehearsed Tuesday through Friday evenings, and we wouldn't be taking our show on the road for another three weeks. I thought we could wait that long, so I postponed the trip home. After all, who else could take my place on the piano bench?

But cancer doesn't care much about trivialities such as road show schedules. When my sister Lisa called and warned me Mom was deteriorating fast, all that mattered was gathering my daughters and packing for the trip to Utah so we could say good-bye. Brian stayed home and worked, but I drove as fast as I dared, covering the six hundred and eighteen miles with my two precious passengers in the back seat, pushing through the California, Nevada, and Utah deserts toward the blue-shingled roof on Blair Street where my parents had lived since I was in third grade.

By the time I arrived at her bedside to stroke her pale red hair and whisper, "I love you, Mom," she didn't know I was there. Regret gnawed at me for putting church over family and for waiting past the time when we could talk together, past the time she could feel my love and hug her granddaughters.

Dad had set up a double bed for her in my old bedroom right next to the bathroom. He had changed her clothing, spoon-fed her soft foods, and encouraged liquids through bendy straws. He carried her gently to the bath, where he bathed his wife of nearly forty-three years.

She had always loved baths, especially in her big, extra-wide tub. She had discovered the wonder tub secondhand in a newspaper ad and used one of her mom talents to make a trade, for what I'll never know. Then she convinced Dad to push, nudge, and cram it into the one small bathroom that served the house. Its extra width spilled out into the limited floor space. She loved her luxurious tub, even when she had to heat the water on the stove for a magical soak.

Did she relive old times while Dad bathed her in that memory-laden place? Perhaps she recalled the time she and Dad had been driving down State Street with a "new" piece of used carpeting protruding from the trunk of their car, which they had just gleaned from a thrift store. At a red light, she had spotted a bigger piece of used carpeting in the bed of the truck next to them, in the color she *really* wanted. She had rolled down her window, then talked the driver of the truck into pulling over and swapping carpets.

Or maybe she had remembered going out searching on a snowy Christmas Eve, taking a puppy from our dog's litter, and trading it for our tree.

Only Mom. The *I Love Lucy* in my life.

I helped Dad bathe her with bubble bath lacing the water, this rag doll of a mom who used to bathe me. After Dad carried her back to her bed, we put her clean garments on and dressed her, and I inhaled her smell of lilac bubble bath like the lilacs that burst out in profusion each spring in the front of their home. And the lilac smell kept the smell of death away, one day at a time.

Her body melted down to skin and bone, making it hard to touch her without causing pain, as no tissue remained to cushion the nerves. One day as I lay on the bed next to her with one of my grandma's hand-stitched quilts covering her frail body, I turned, touching her slightly. She hollered out with more energy than I thought was left inside her body's tiny shell, "Gee Rethsejane! I sure get murtalized a lot lately!"

Dad and I looked at each other in shock. She hadn't spoken in weeks. These were the last words she ever spoke to me—her favorite Mormon cuss words, combined with an entirely new verb she conjugated on her deathbed. I know if she could have chosen her last words, they would have been different ones, so I smile. Only Mom. Last words full of spunk.

Through my tears, I was sure she'd forgiven me for not arriving sooner. After all, hadn't she taught me to accept Church callings and to always keep promises? But even so, how did I forgive myself? I learned the hard way that promises of love should always go before promises of work.

The mistake I made with my mom, I won't repeat with Cindy. I still have time. Each evening, I go to my friend's house, where she lies in her king-sized suite in their large custom home. I pull up a vanity chair or sit on the edge of her bed as my fingers seek out sore spots in her feet and calves. We talk, share, and care. Sometimes we laugh or trade secrets. As some of her pain lessens, the pain in my heart heals.

But there are things I don't share with Cindy. Big things. I don't tell her of the doctrinal problems I'm discovering in Church history. I don't tell her how it's threatening to drain everything I believe in. Although a part of me feels like a fraud holding these back from my friend, this doesn't feel like the place or time. I know she doesn't have much time left.

Cindy continues to decline. I know their son Dallin, still on his mission in Spain, won't see his mom alive unless he comes home early from his mission. Missionaries sometimes aren't even allowed to go home for the funeral of a parent, and I want more for Cindy. Dallin needs to be home to hug his mother before it's too late, because I know what too late feels like.

I have to do what I can, although my position as a woman holds little power. I call our bishop and try to impress upon him the urgency of the situation—Cindy doesn't have long.

"Please, Bishop Zone. Her son needs to come home."

Her son does return home, released early from his mission. I don't know if my conversation with our bishop has a smidgen to do with it, for after all, those are priesthood decisions, always made by the men.

A small cove in my mind would like to think my bishop heard me and was influenced in some small way to bring her son home while it still mattered to both of them, but later I'll read the following statement in the Church Missionary Handbook, and my heart will break at the harsh reality of the Church's official policy.

> If a member of a missionary's immediate family dies, the Church encourages the missionary to remain in the field. However, if the family insists that the missionary return home, the missionary may be allowed to return at the family's expense. The stake president may request such an exception through the Missionary Department. (p. 99)

When Cindy slips into a coma, her family moves her to a convalescent center. One day her husband asks me if I can give the family a short reprieve from their constant vigil. Of course. This will give me a last chance to be with her. But when I enter the room, the air hangs heavy with the pungent smell of antiseptics, and the pale, frail person I see lying on the stark white sheets of the hospital bed looks nothing like my friend.

Within a week, the joy of knowing Cindy crawls to a conclusion, and she's gone.

Days before her funeral, Amy and Charlene, two other of her close friends, ask if I'll go to the mortuary with them to help dress her body for burial. Since members who have gone to the temple are buried in their temple clothing to be ready for the resurrection, Cindy must be prepared.

Amy tells us, "Dressing the body is considered an ordinance. For us to show proper respect, we should all wear our Sunday clothes." So the three of us, all decked out in our Sunday-go-to-meeting dresses, heels, and hose, climb in Charlene's new Mustang for the eighty-mile trip to Forest Lawn Mortuary.

When we arrive, we meet two of Cindy's daughters, who have also come to help dress her. They are both wearing jeans. I imagine Cindy gets quite a kick watching us worry over how we're dressed while we dress her body.

The Mormon mortician has already placed the white temple garments on her. We add her other ceremonial temple clothing, except for the temple veil, which her husband will pull down over her face just before the casket lid is shut. Although I've asked, I still haven't been told why women veil their faces in the temple and in their coffins, and the men don't.

We do our best to dress Cindy properly for resurrection morning. She's wearing her garments, temple clothing, coiffed hair, and makeup, just as she always did in life. She's ready for her final journey.

When I think of Cindy, I also think of my mom. Although they were separated by age, economics, and miles, they were both strong women who both generally got their own way. And I loved them both so much. I'm glad I was there for Cindy at the end of her life, but oh, if only I could have been there in time to do the same for my mom.

Faith versus work—the age-old battle. Mormons value works, saying faith will follow. But when the life of a loved one is ending, only love can direct us home. Works might get the job done, faith might hold on tight, but only love says, "Someone else must play the piano while I'm driving home to see my mother, and my children's grandmother, for the last time."

TWENTY

THE SWAMPLANDS
1997

*S*ea-foam green dazzles through the fluted glass cups and swirls around the rippled edges of the matching plates. The crystal wonders perch atop a cluttered display in a local antique shop, until I hear them sing out to me from the confusion of assorted bric-a-brac. Not that I need new dishes. My cupboards bulge with sets purchased over twenty-four years of marriage, plus those handed down from my mom. But there's just something about this color.

"Ring 'em up!" I impulsively tell the clerk.

Since then, every time I spy them in my cupboard, they pull my thoughts far from my desert home toward a sparkling sea the same rich shade of green. Maybe one day I can live in a place like that. But not this day.

Today, my youngest daughter sets out my green plates at fleet speed so she can change from her Sunday dress into her favorite blue jeans. Both her older sisters are already in their bedroom changing, giggling, and probably sharing intimate secrets on which she's missing out.

On this particular day, as I inhale the aroma of the Sunday roast I'm basting, I have no more idea of that faraway shining sea than I do of the reality of a swampland that separates me from it, but two calls from a ringing phone will soon change it all.

The first call comes with an impatient jingle. Not realizing the events I'm setting into motion, I grab the phone.

"Lorelei, this is Jen," says a cheerful voice. "Are you coming to the Big Bear Singles' Conference?"

I haven't known her long, but already Jen shines out as a new definition of hero to me, the legendary driving force behind this upcoming conference. She has stepped up to do what no one else would and year after year has put in all the tilling, toiling, and tugging required to keep the conference going.

"You bet I am," I answer, dropping my basting spoon into the sink with a clatter. Although the conference is months away, I already have the dates circled in red on my calendar.

"Great, I'm glad. I've heard good things about your teaching the Gospel Doctrine [adult scripture] class," she continues, "and I'd like you to be one of our Sunday sacrament meeting speakers."

My insides do cartwheels. She wants *me* to speak at the singles' conference! I try to tone down the excitement in my voice and sound causal.

"Of course."

"And can you invite two priesthood leaders to speak with you? And get back to me with their names for the program?"

"You got it, Jen," I answer. A simple request. What could go wrong?

"Okay, good. One more thing. The scripture, 'Angels Round About,' that you told me you put to music? We'd like to use it for the theme of our conference and have you perform it."

I can hardly breathe with the excitement welling up inside me. "Absolutely. I'll play the piano and ask my friend Glenda to sing it."

My mind races. This singles' conference will be the best ever.

Little did I know. That one phone call, holding only the best of intentions to promote the conference we affectionately call the Home of the Big Bear Hug, will blow up in all our faces.

Everything about this fall annual conference shouts excitement to me— from the rustic cabins we stay in at the Church-owned campground, to the barbecue and western dance that kick things off Friday night, the breakfast aromas that pull us out of bed Saturday morning, the classes offered on the ups and downs of being single Mormons, the dinner we all devour while checking out who showed up that year, and my favorite part—the highlight—the Saturday night dance. Church services will be held bright and early Sunday morning, and then Jen will already be busy planning next year's conference.

The Church-sponsored conference offers the wonderful possibility to meet someone special, like a massive fishing net filled with new opportunities, all in one fun-packed weekend.

I waste no time making an appointment to talk with my bishop. When I ask him to speak, I know he'll have to leave our congregation that Sunday, arrange substitutes in several meetings, and drive the hour and a half to Big Bear. Can he do all this? As I watch his face for clues, he flashes a quick smile and with his firm handshake seals the deal. Yes!

Next, I make an appointment to meet with Brother Atchison, the High Councilman over single members. He seems a logical choice because of his stewardship over the singles, but when I ask him, he hesitates. During his long hesitation, I can't help but notice, as I do whenever I see him in the foyer, how his weak features are less than flattering on a man. I know he has a passel of kids at home, and I hope they don't take after him. He projects harshness that doesn't match his features, and although I'm sure he must love his forever family, I wonder how often his stiffness can soften into a hug for those kids.

His flat reply interrupts my thoughts. "I'll have to get back to you on that."

Three weeks later, I set out only one sea-foam green plate. Its comforting hue matches the color of tropical seas, calmer seas. Seas where dolphins leap and fishes swim, a place full of fantasy, fins, and fun, which contrasts sharply with this Sunday as my girls are with their dad. And his girlfriend.

I hate my girls being gone. The house sequesters me in stillness. The *tick-tick-tick* of the family room clock makes the only sound against the emptiness that clings to the walls, loneliness imbedded in coats of semi-gloss. How long have those deep-textured walls felt so cold? I try to remember when they surrounded me with warmth and happiness, but I can't.

The phone rings, distracting me from my quiet house. I yank it off its cradle.

"This is Brother Atchison," the male voice announces. "I'm calling about the singles' conference."

Giving me no time to respond, he continues, "I won't be speaking at the conference. I could have told you sooner, but I debated whether I should tell you the real reason."

What?

"Sacrament Meeting is a function of the priesthood and should only be directed by priesthood men. It is inappropriate for a woman to handle speaking assignments and especially to ask a priesthood bearer, such as myself, to speak."

The words ooze from his mouth as easily as dark oil diffusing over seawater heading indifferently toward a sandy beach.

"So I won't be speaking at the conference," he concludes, "because I'm *offended* a woman is issuing the invitation."

Offended? The phone begins to shake in my hand, and I back up against the kitchen counter.

"You're telling me," I manage in a low whisper, "you won't speak at the conference because of my . . . genitals?"

I feel my face burning hot with humiliation.

"No, not . . . well, actually, yes," he admits. "It's unacceptable for a woman to have asked me. It's very clear in the patriarchal order of the Church that *only* priesthood men are to preside."

I say nothing.

"And, I'm telling you, you are not to ask another priesthood leader to participate, either." Now Brother Atchison's tone of superiority sharpens. "Give me the name of the sister who is acting in charge of this conference. She is also out of line."

I'd love to be able to say otherwise, but obedience wins over valor, and in shock, I offer up Jen's name.

Although I don't know it, by being a woman and having the gall to ask a priesthood man to speak, I'm setting perilous consequences in motion. As I hang up the phone, somewhere, an arrogant alligator rolls over in smelly swamp waters. He glories in his dominion, just like Brother Atchison, who now stalks his newest victim, the Big Bear Singles' Conference. Before another year makes its rounds, he'll seize our beloved conference in a spinning death roll, and crush it.

My legs wobble as I stumble toward my dining table and sit down. Glancing at my lone green plate, a fleeting thought shoots through my mind of another kind of place—a place with green tropical seas, where mermaids ride the backs of porpoises and shriek with the joy of being alive. A soothing, gentle place, where heart matters more than genitalia.

But does such a place really exist? And if so, is there a way I can get there?

TWENTY-ONE

FROZEN
1997

I like snow.

I like the big fat flakes that settle in for the long haul on pine tree limbs, the sloppy wet ones that expire after hitting the damp grass, even the ones taken hostage by sludgy roadside snowbanks that are released only when tires go squishing through them. Snow reminds me of growing up in the city known for its salty lake and accompanies many of the big events in my life.

My daughters' snow education comes mostly from visits to their grandparents in Utah, but every once in a lucky while, our desert community will be covered with the crystal-white stuff. I always keep warm mittens in the hall closet just in case enough of the fluff falls for us to be able to chase each other around the yard, tossing snowballs.

No snow falls this particular Christmas season, however. Not a flake in the sky. Although a cold wind blows around each chimney and fence post, I scarcely notice.

Nevertheless, I feel a hearty dose of holiday spirit. "Come to a Christmas party at my house!" I say, inviting all the single members for a December Family Home Evening. Our singles' group considers each other family, and I have been called as the singles' representative.

"Welcome, and come on in," I greet each of the more than forty people who crowd into my home for the yuletide bash. This far exceeds the dozen or so people who usually show up for the monthly gatherings. We feast on turkey dripping with gravy, baked yams with marshmallow topping, and every holiday treat my table can hold. As an extra surprise, Santa jingles in with his red velvet bag brimming with gifts.

As the evening winds down, I add another surprise. "Come on, everyone. Let's head over to the bishop's house and sing carols for his family. You come too, Santa. I'm sure there are still presents left in your bag for his children!"

Fast-forward to February fourteen months later. The phone rings and my youngest daughter hauls the cordless phone into the bathroom. I'm relaxing in my ritual bubble bath after a long day of caring for children. Trust me, I need lots of bubble baths these days. Darlene, a friend from the singles program, is on the line.

"Brother Atchison told me to call you," she says, her tone heavy with apology, "and give you a message."

Oh geez, my favorite bubble interrupter.

She continues, "Remember the Christmas party you held for the singles over a year ago?"

"Yes, of course I remember."

She hesitates. "You're never supposed to do that again."

"Never do what again?" I ask. "Have a party in my home?"

"Well, no. That's not quite it."

"Then *what*? It couldn't be about budget, because I paid for everything myself, even all the gifts." My hand whisks away some renegade bubbles from the phone. "What could I have possibly done wrong?"

"You were in charge of it," she says.

"Of course I was in charge of it," I say, perturbed now. "I did everything. That's why it was such a success. What's this all about, anyway?"

"You were supposed to have a man in charge. I mean, have a priesthood man in charge."

The silence between us thickens. I'm not sure who is most uncomfortable. After all, she's just the unfortunate messenger. A woman messenger, as it happens, on an errand for a priesthood-holding male who is too barnacle-clad to make such an absurd call himself.

In other words, permission is granted for me to offer my home, plan the party, clean the house, put up the tree, cook the turkey, arrange for Santa, rent his costume, and buy all the presents, but the official task of welcoming everyone must be done by—a *man*.

And, permission is also granted for me to greet the guests, take their coats, make them comfortable, mix the punch, serve the food, coordinate the gifts, launch the games, and ensure fun for everyone, but, at the conclusion of the party, to thank the guests for coming, I must once again turn things over to—a *man*.

Then, of course, I can clean the house again.

A chill surrounds me that even the bubbles can't warm as we end the call.

Although there has been no snow outside again this year, I can hear a cold February wind howling around each corner of the house. I shiver and splash the heated water over myself as I vow that was the last Church Christmas party, or any other kind of Church party, I'll ever host.

Yet, deep down, I know the bottom line is—and always will be—truth. So even if at times I find my religion frustrating as all tarnation, if Mormonism is true, in Mormonism I belong, and in Mormonism I will stay.

But a crack is spreading through my cherished Mormon truth. I've heard it said you can always tell who set the rules by noticing whom those rules benefit, and it's becoming crystal clear whom the Mormon rules benefit.

As Susan B. Anthony put it, "I distrust those people who know so well what God wants them to do, because I notice it always coincides with their own desires."

A question begins chafing at me. Is this really the way God wants us to live, with the man always on top? Or is it just that the rules are all made by men?

TWENTY-TWO

SINKHOLE OF FAITH
Or, as a friend said to me recently,
"Someone must have told you truth matters."
1996 - 1998

S tunned. That's how my old dolphin sidekicks Thought and Logic react
when Bishop Zone calls me, a woman, and a divorced woman at that,
to teach the scripture class for adults called Gospel Doctrine.

I can't wait to call and tell my dad! Then I remember—he's gone. I shiver
a little as a great wave of longing for him surges over me. How I miss our tradition of talking about scriptures, ideas, and doctrine, and I'll miss it even
more as I prepare the upcoming lessons.

"Yes," I tell my bishop. Of course I say yes. Never in my entire life have
I said no, as we're taught these callings come from God and are just channeled
through our bishops. Some callings aren't as great as others, I must admit, like
being called as a nursery leader, but this one is quite a big deal. I shouldn't even
have a thought like that in my head, but I admit I do. I quickly add, "I'll do
my best," as both my dolphin friends do back flips.

But never in my wildest imagination could I know that by doing my best
to follow my bishop, I'd create the waves of transformation that lay ahead.

Our course of study will rotate through the four standard scriptures of
the Church: Book of Mormon, *Doctrine & Covenants* (revelations of Joseph
Smith), Old Testament, and New Testament. Half of the scriptures we study
are familiar to the rest of Christianity, with the other half courtesy of Joseph
Smith for some tangy Mormon flavor.

When I begin teaching the class midyear, we're already halfway through the Book of Mormon. Like most Mormons, I'm most familiar with our signature scripture. I've read it many times, once even in *Español* with an English-to-Spanish dictionary propped up close by just to prove I could do it. It took me a *very* long time.

With the same intensity I've put into all my previous callings from any of my bishops, I spend ten hours a week studying for each of my Sunday lessons. If I were to read only the verses within the reading assignment my Gospel Doctrine manual refers to, I wouldn't learn as much as I do, but I read and study *all* of the chapters, skipping nothing. This ends up making all the difference.

I also sign up for Critical Thinking at the local junior college, because— who's the greatest critical thinker of all? That would be God, of course. So if I learn the principles of critical thinking, won't it help me better understand and comprehend God's will, discover hidden secrets of the universe, and unlock the mysteries of the scriptures? That's the plan.

A few years later when I'll teach the Old Testament, more accurately termed the Hebrew Bible, I'll also sign up for a class on the Old Testament. As I'll study, I'll come to understand why many of these stories are never preached over the pulpits in Sunday school. Although I will find notable exceptions, many of the stories between Genesis's "In the beginning" and Malachi's ending "lest I come and smite the earth with a curse" are too graphic and barbaric to be considered uplifting. Most are not stories your children should be told at bedtime. Or anytime.

For me, the worst parts will be the number of human sacrifices and the continual slaughtering of nations in the name of God. I'll find these chapters difficult to even read through, but read through them I will. For my class each Sunday, however, I'll sift through the mayhem and find something uplifting, such as prophets, psalms, and even a prophetess or two to discuss and bring hope and faith into our lives.

When the year of studying the Old Testament finally comes to a close, I'll be thrilled to know next year we'll be studying the New Testament. Hallelujah! We'll be through with human sacrifice.

Christmas is just a few months away, and I thumb through my teacher's manual to get a look at the lesson. I admit I've had a love/hate relationship with this manual for some time because after I study the scriptures, I sometimes arrive at different conclusions. But for Christmas, I'm sure we'll be on the same page.

I flip forward, find the lesson, and read the title: "Follow the Prophet." So just days before Christmas, the Church wants Gospel Doctrine teachers the world over to teach about following the prophet instead of our Savior, Jesus Christ?

Holy mackerel.

Who really leads this church, anyway?

Our year of studying the Book of Mormon is complete, and we're ready to begin our study of the *Doctrine and Covenants*, which is composed of Joseph Smith's revelations. I continue to pore over each scripture assignment, immerse myself in Church history, and wade through Church commentaries, including antique copies inherited from my father. I find I'm thrown into nasty tailspins as I discover how many historical accounts are changed to reflect the Church's official story line.

Both of my steadfast companions, Thought and Logic, swim loyally by my side as challenge after doctrinal challenge comes hurtling my way.

How do I deal with, for example, the number of different accounts Joseph gave of his First Vision? These include his handwritten account saying an angel appeared to him, another account saying Jesus appeared to him, and yet another account (now the official version), claiming that two personages, father and son, appeared to him in a grove of trees. After such a glorious experience, didn't he know which, or even how many, had thrown back the heavenly veil and announced their holy selves?

Also, according to David Whitmer, one of the Three Witnesses quoted in the introduction to the Book of Mormon, Joseph Smith didn't even look at the golden plates to translate them. Instead, he peered into a black hat and watched magical letters flicker to form words, which he then dictated to his scribe, Oliver Cowdry.

What? A black hat? Why did God go to all this trouble of having the plates inscribed hundreds of years ago, having the prophet Moroni hide them in a hillside in upstate New York, and leading the boy Joseph Smith to their location hidden under a rock, when they weren't even required to bring forth the Book of Mormon? Then to complicate matters for the skeptics, He had Moroni take them back into the heavens.

I'm desperate for answers.

And after Joseph had already married Emma, he propositioned other young women for marriage. He promised them that if they accepted, he would personally guarantee their entire family would enter into the highest Mormon heaven. Even more bewildering, many of the women added to his marital fold were already married to other men, including some of his dearest and closest friends, a lusty example of what Susan B. Anthony warned us against.

Help!

I want to be the best Mormon I can be, and because I've been taught to follow our leaders, I begin searching more current information about Church history. In horror, I find that in 1981, Apostle Boyd K. Packer insisted on keeping Church history docked and locked right where the Church wanted it. He warned the Church historians at the annual Church Educational System Religious Educators Symposium: "There is a temptation for the writer or the teacher of Church history to want to tell everything, whether it is worthy or faith-promoting or not. Some things that are true are not very useful."

Especially when the truth hurts.

My instructor's manual tells me to "bear my testimony" each week and to include my witness to the truthfulness of the gospel of Jesus Christ, of Joseph Smith being a prophet of God, and of our present prophet, Gordon B. Hinkley, being a prophet of God.

As the doctrinal problems mount each week, this becomes tougher. I can't testify about something I'm struggling to still believe myself, but if I don't, what kind of an example am I? I must juggle honesty with my class and myself.

I concoct my strategy. As I close each lesson, I say, "Brothers and sisters, our prophet tells us to study the scriptures daily. I testify to you, that if you follow this counsel, scripture study can change your life. It has changed mine."

I just don't say in which direction.

One Sunday morning as I'm getting dressed for church, a tempting idea jumps into my head.

Why not? I give right in, and instead of reaching for my church garments, I put on a pretty leopard-spotted bra and panties that sit lonely in a dresser drawer. As I button up my modest Sunday suit over them, I double-check in the mirror that the spots don't show through my white linen skirt so no one could suspect my secret.

Now standing in front of my class, I'm charged with a strange feeling of elation, as if an imposter Lorelei, formerly unrevealed, is teaching the class. I almost blush as I recall the times many years ago after Brian and I had gone to the temple that I would come home from work and change from my garments into sexy little outfits for him. Thank heavens the class members don't know about my prior backsliding. That unapproved behavior of mine lasted for the better part of a year, until I put a stop to it when the guilt caught up with me.

But I know today's transgression is a one-time radical act, and next week I'll be back to wearing the officially-sanctioned Mormon underwear while I teach gospel principles. Does any other woman in America feel outrageous for wearing normal pretty underwear? Maybe not, but just for today, I experience a strange exhilaration.

I'll soon discover that the challenges I've met pale in comparison, however, to my biggest problem, the mother lode of all icebergs I could crash into, which lies straight ahead. And it's part of a traveling mummy show.

As the story goes, in 1835, a Michael H. Chandler toured the Mormon settlement of Kirkland, Ohio, with four Egyptian mummies and several rolls of papyrus that, alas, no one could translate. Enter our hero, Joseph Smith. The man with the reputation of translating golden plates obtained the parchments, proclaimed them a historical treasure written "by Abraham's own hand," and translated them.

Problem solved.

This translation is hailed as the Book of Abraham (part of the Pearl of Great Price), and the Church canonizes it as part of its official scriptures in 1880. Church leaders thought the papyrus that Joseph Smith translated had burned in the Chicago fire of 1871. But in 1966, it surfaced in the Metropolitan Museum of Art, complete with a bill of sale from his wife, Emma Smith. Uh-oh. Now modern-day experts with modern-day knowledge and equipment can examine it—and examine it they do.

Problems just beginning.

Egyptologists immediately proclaimed it a typical funeral papyrus that commonly accompanies mummies—not a handwritten story by Abraham, not a philosophy to enlighten our day, not a historical find as Joseph said. Instead, it was a simple, common, Egyptian funeral text.

When the papyrus was discovered in 1966, it was a telling event for the Church, a banner year for the Beatles, and my junior year at BYU. Although I might have been humming the Beatles' hit "Do You Want to Know a Secret" all the way to Provo, I would have been blown out of the water if I had known about the secret I'd stumble across years later—a secret that would alter the course of my life.

Now, thirty years later, I've uncovered it.

Logic isn't smiling. In fact, his long, pointed face grimaces as he swims by. The waters churn around me as I tackle everything I can find on the subject, but the more I study, the more my head aches. Logic swims in frantic circles, doing aquatic gymnastics as we search for any plausible explanation.

Meanwhile, Thought begs for an answer that could keep me in Mormonism. He constructs hoops of hope to jump through—hoops such as, "Could God have inscribed multiple layers of truth in the funeral texts? Could it not only be a funeral text but, on some spiritual level, also be the writing of Abraham?"

But there's one damnable problem with this: Joseph Smith said the papyrus was written by Abraham "in his own hand," not recopied later. Logic can't ignore the young age of the papyrus. No way is it old enough to date back to Abraham's time. Simply put, Abraham's hand could not have written on papyrus that wouldn't come into existence until centuries after his death.

So if the Book of Abraham proves to be a fraud, what about the Book of Mormon? Heck, what about Joseph Smith himself? I'm already having a hard enough time standing up in front of this class each Sunday. What about my fifty years in Mormonism as the only True Church? What about my forever family?

I've come to this, crouched on my bathroom floor, my head propped over the toilet, my stomach roiling as the worst migraine of my life explodes between my temples. Over the throbbing inside my head, I hear my daughters' anxious voices calling from my bedroom, "Mom, are you ready for Family Home Evening? It's your turn to read tonight."

I panic, trying to focus on their question. They grow restless, waiting to share our weekly Monday night reading, a fictionalized nine-volume account of the history of the Mormon Church called The Work and the Glory. How ironic. More fiction exists in my religious life than I ever suspected.

Coldness soaks into my knees from the bathroom floor and rushes quickly into my stomach, where disbelief and fear swirl in a vortex. Finally, I can no longer hold back the nasty tide and begin heaving, throwing up the religion I've lived with for fifty years. The pounding and pulsing throb through me as I retch my old belief system into the toilet bowl. Here in my bathroom, on my knees, I regurgitate my faith.

I lift my chin, my head still pounding as the ramifications rush over me. The question that scares me the most is—what in the hell can I tell my daughters?

TWENTY-THREE

TIDE'S A-CHANGING
1998

*T*all. Stocky. Good looking. Over six feet tall. Seems even taller next to his wife, who barely breaks five. Recently returned from his mission when they met in college. She also dreamed of going on a mission, but he told her he wouldn't wait if she went. So they married. Babies. Soon. Three, four, five. He, not she, continues education. Successful in career—accountant to business owner. Successful at Church—moving on up. Obviously, God's blessing them. Still, bills stack up faster than one income supporting seven people can pay. Bankruptcy.

Yet always hard-working. And friendly.

Bishop Zone, my bishop.

Like his counterparts around the world, Bishop Zone isn't paid for his Church service. Rather, he works full time supporting his young family, then spends his evenings and weekends serving other Church members. On top of all this, he pays ten percent of his income, like the rest of the ward members, and has his garage stuffed full of wheat in case of an emergency, like the rest of the ward members.

Although bishops don't get paid for their service, the high-ranking general authorities of the Church do. As an example of church reimbursement, mission presidents, high-up in the Mormon hierarchy, receive full reimbursement for all expenses, including rent, medical, utilities, food, clothing, housekeeping, even gardening.

Not bad for volunteer work.

For their dependent children up to age twenty-six, mission presidents receive reimbursement for all elementary and secondary school, undergraduate university tuition, missions, even extracurricular activities, such as music and dance lessons.

On top of this, because they're "unsalaried," they're exempt from paying income tax on any of these reimbursements. The Mission President Handbook says straight out: "If you are required to file an income-tax report for other purposes, do not list any funds you receive from the Church, regardless of where you serve or where you hold citizenship." (p. 82)

Because Church finances aren't made public, nor is this handbook, most members don't realize the extent of payments that the authorities at the top receive. Even I am shocked to read in the same handbook, "The amount of any funds reimbursed to you should be kept strictly confidential and should not be discussed with missionaries, other mission presidents, friends, or family members." (p. 80)

The following statement from the handbook crystalizes the financial policy of the Mormon Church: "Never represent in any way that you are paid for your service." (p. 82)

This strict secrecy of Mormon finances stands stark in comparison with other religions that have no hesitation sharing their financial information.

A Mormon man I meet online from Arizona becomes incensed when I mention that top Church leaders get paid. I understand why he bristles. In the temple, we're taught that a Church with a paid ministry is of the devil and that a sign of the True Church is *not* having a paid ministry. But apparently, this just applies to the majority in the lower ranks, because the guys higher up, well, they get paid.

But Bishop Zone's efforts are strictly volunteered. I respect my bishop, although I wonder if he has a shrimp-sized inkling of the challenges a single Mormon woman faces. Figuring there's only one way to find out, I make an appointment with him. Besides, there are other things I want to talk about.

As I drive to the church, a hot afternoon wind blows under a fired-up desert sun, raising havoc all around my neighborhood. Thoughts are also racing wildly in my head, including the memory of a member telling me, "Your problem is you think too much." Whoa! The solution to my doctrinal dilemmas is to just not think about them? I hold out higher hopes for my bishop.

As I climb out of my car, the wind gusts about me as I make a run for the church doors. Rushing through the flurry, I ask myself if coming here to meet with him is the right thing. But once I'm inside his office, he welcomes me with a firm handshake, and I hope for the best.

He listens as I tell him about priesthood men being offended when I asked a man to speak in Sacrament Meeting, by how I danced at a church social, and how I held a Christmas party. I tell him about places where my Gospel Doctrine manual doesn't match up with the scriptures, places where the official history has been altered, and places where scriptures are purposely misinterpreted to support Church views.

He still listens.

I also tell him of doctrinal problems I'm uncovering while I study each week to prepare my lesson. One of the most damnable is how Joseph Smith wrote in his *Lectures of Faith* (formerly canonized Mormon scripture) that God the Father was a spirit, Jesus Christ had a body, and the Holy Ghost was the mind of both. (*Lectures on Faith*, Lecture Fifth, paragraph 2, pp. 54-55).

And this was after Joseph's First Vision where he *saw* God the Father and Jesus Christ? *Saw* their bodies as they spoke with him? Then later he said, "God is a spirit"? That's Protestantism, not Mormonism. (The Mormon Church doesn't claim to be Protestant, as these churches grew out of the Reformation protesting the Catholic Church, but instead claims a divine restoration by Joseph Smith.)

To this last dilemma, Bishop Zone says, "I don't know the answer. It's not like we're comparing apples and oranges. This is Joseph Smith against Joseph Smith."

It might not be a great answer, but at least it's an honest one. Although we talk a long time, I wonder if I'm making any headway. Can my bishop see the magnitude of the doctrinal problems we discuss? Or the huge Mormon undercurrent of oppression toward women? And if so, can he make any difference? After all, since the men are in charge, they have the God-given right, duty even, to make sure the women remain in their proper shore-hugging place.

By the time I leave his office, I know my speaking out hasn't changed anything in the Mormon hierarchy, maybe hasn't even changed anything in my bishop's mind. Even so, something inside me has changed, and I notice things outside have also changed. The hot wind has settled into a cooling breeze, and the sunlight has sunk from sight, replaced by a pearl-toned crescent moon that sails slowly across the sky, spilling its soft feminine light over me all the way home.

TWENTY-FOUR

SWINGING ON A STAR
1999

*D*oes God have a wife?

If you're a Mormon, He does. She's our Heavenly Mother who sits beside Heavenly Father, and the two of them together created us—the biblical way, if you happen to be interested in those kinds of details.

But that's about as good as the news gets, because even if I, as a Mormon, want to talk about Her or acknowledge Her in my prayers, I can get in trouble. *Big* trouble.

In fact, several important Mormon women have had their memberships yanked out from under them for that very sin. Some were part of the September Six, a term coined by the news media for a Church "purge" of well-known intellectuals in September of 1993. Maxine Hanks, a feminist theologian, was excommunicated for her book *Women and Authority*, thus being on too familiar terms writing about this Mother in whom we doctrinally believe. Lynne Whitesides, President of the Mormon Women's Forum, was disfellowshipped, which is almost as bad as being excommunicated, and told not to talk *any more* about Heavenly Mother.

In 1995, Gail Houston, an English professor at Brigham Young University, was fired for writing articles about praying to Heavenly Mother. Also that year, Janice Merrill Allred and Margaret Merrill Toscano found themselves hauled into Church courts and excommunicated for writing about and discussing God the Mother.

Since we doctrinally believe in this Mother, wouldn't it make sense to be able to talk or write about Her? After all, the Catholics get to pray to the Virgin Mary to validate the divine feminine. But Church power and authority stay solidly with the men in the bass section, and never ascends to the women with those lilting soprano voices.

Better women than I have fussed about this and paid the price, but my turn shows up anyway. I hear about a woman's conference being held at the University of Utah in Salt Lake City, and I submit a paper to present. When it's accepted, I make the trip to speak, but I'm uneasy speaking under my real name since the Church has started keeping close tabs on its members and our activities.

Someone might question how the Church can possibly monitor all its members. After all, it's a worldwide church, so keeping tabs on all of us can't be an easy job. It would take a separate branch of the Church, an agency like the FBI, to do something like that.

Which is exactly why the Church organized the Strengthening Church Members Committee.

Cross my seaworthy heart, it's the truth. This committee keeps track of everyone they think might be out of line, cause a threat, or need to be "strengthened" by their Church leaders. To accomplish this, the Church started a file on individual members who trigger their suspicions. According to Mormon Apostle Boyd K Packer, (May 18, 1993), the members the Church consider its biggest threats are feminists, gays, and intellectuals. Especially those damn intellectuals.

What actions could start the file-creation process? Even as a member, I can only guess. Maybe it's just as well. Knowing too many of the rules that govern my membership in the Lord's One True Church, and thus my eternal salvation, could be hazardous to my faith.

All I can say is, once such a file is in place and the undercurrent of suspicion causes the scales to tip, watch out below. At that point, the unfortunate singled-out member will be "warned." Although the warning comes from on high, meaning Salt Lake City, it's delivered locally. The warning can be friendly or serious. The singled-out member sometimes receives the ultimate "strengthening"—excommunication.

This secret organization to spy on the Church's own members has been around since 1985, when Prophet Ezra Taft Benson formed it soon after he became the sixteenth prophet, but since it was secret, hardly anyone knew about it. In fact, it was only when the Utah-based newspaper *The Salt Lake*

Tribune leaked its existence in 1992 that the word officially got out. Once that torpedo hit, a First Presidency spokesman finally fessed up, and newspapers across the nation ran the story about the Mormon Church and its "secret files." Pretty newsworthy stuff.

But since I know about this committee, even though I live three states away from Utah, in California, I know how far the Church's tentacles of control spread. I don't want to take any chances, so I speak under the assumed name of Valerie Fairchild. I wonder if there's a file on *her*.

I call my presentation:

Playing with Dolls
A Look at Mormon Theology Concerning Women

When I was a little girl, I loved playing with dolls—dolls with straight, silky blonde hair; curly-cropped red hair; and baby dolls without any hair. Since my mom collected dolls, there were always plenty at our house. What fun we had with our dolls.

Growing up loving dolls, perhaps it was natural that I accepted a theology of deity based on my experience of playing with dolls.

Let me explain. In my Mormon home, my parents taught me that in heaven, I had been born to Heavenly Father and Heavenly Mother before being born on Earth. Even as a tyke, I could relate to that—it seemed simple and understandable. And being a normal child, within a few years, I asked my parents the next question, "What will become of me after this life is over?"

They explained to me that my brother, since he was a boy, could grow and evolve throughout the eternities and become a god. And since I was a girl, I could grow and evolve throughout the eternities and become a wife of god. And if I actually achieved this most exalted state held out to Mormon women, I would eternally produce spirit offspring for my husband/god. Of course, marriage is essential to this plan.

Sounded sensible to me, since I already understood being loved by a mother and father, and I liked playing mother as I played with my dolls.

I didn't worry too much about the implications of the Mormon belief in polygamy. You know, Mormons believe God has many wives who produce His spirit children eternally. Accordingly, I would be just one of God's wives. God would be *very* busy.

As I grew, I learned more of the doctrine concerning God and His wives. Sitting in Sacrament meeting with my family, I would sing the familiar hymn,

"O My Father" written by Eliza R. Snow, a plural wife of both Joseph Smith and Brigham Young. This hymn is meaningful, especially to the women, and controversial, especially to the brethren.

> In the heav'ns are parents single?
> No, the thought makes reason stare!
> Truth is reason, truth eternal
> Tells me I've a mother there.
>
> When I leave this frail existence,
> When I leave this mortal by,
> Father, Mother, may I meet you
> In your royal courts on high?
>
> Then, at length, when I've completed
> All you sent me forth to do,
> With your mutual approbation
> Let me come and dwell with you.

I liked the idea of having a Mother and Father in heaven, just like my own mother and father on Earth.

In Primary—the organization for children—I was taught that a woman's ultimate glory in this life and in the eternities consists of her role with her children. Thus, the Mormon glory held out to me was being a mother in this life and a mother in the afterlife. There, I would endlessly produce and care for spirit children who would later be physically born onto other earths. This would be the ultimate reward for living a righteous life, being obedient to the commandments, being married in the temple for eternity, and, of course, following the counsel of the brethren.

In Mutual—the organization for young women—I was taught we had existed eternally before coming here to Earth, and we would exist eternally in the afterlife, and as small as this period of mortality is when compared with the eternal nature of our existence—*everything*, including which kingdom of glory we obtain—depends on how well we do here.

I began to notice during these meetings that our Eternal Mother was rarely referred to, unless we sang that hymn. And I began to question and wonder, wouldn't a wife of God be a goddess? Wouldn't She have another function in addition to producing children? Wouldn't God our Mother be more than an impregna-*tee*? After all, God our Father was more than an impregna-*tor*. He did other things, like creating new worlds and galaxies. Would She ever do more than just play with Her dolls?

With disappointment, I heard on April 5, 1991, that Gordon B. Hinckley, then first counselor in the First Presidency and later prophet, said he considered it inappropriate for anyone in the Church to pray to our Mother in Heaven. He stated as basis for this that he found "nowhere in the Standard Works an account where Jesus prayed other than to His Father in Heaven . . . I have looked in vain for any instance . . . [of] 'a prayer to our Mother in Heaven.'"

Although I have to question how long he actually spent searching the scriptures to realize this, I thought this line of reasoning was valid. I too have searched the scriptures and found—contrary to accepted church doctrine—nowhere where it says Christ was married. I too have looked in vain. Therefore—contrary to accepted Church doctrine—I remain single.

So we aren't supposed to pray to our Mother, even though She has achieved the ultimate glory for a Mormon woman. While we are on Earth—where *everything* depends on our choices—we are not to pray to Her, we pray only to Him. During Her children's time on Earth, She has no power or influence. When it really counts—*She* doesn't.

I wondered, if Mother God's role doesn't include being involved with Her children in mortality—apparently, this is reserved for Father God—She must have been involved with them in the pre-existence. With this in mind, I was happy to read in "A Proclamation to the World—The Family" (issued by the Church in 1995) that we are born of heavenly parents. Sounded to me like this validates our relationship with our Heavenly Mother.

But my enthusiasm quickly vanished when I read the next paragraph: "In the premortal realm, spirit sons and daughters knew and worshiped God as their eternal Father." Wait a minute. God only includes the Father? We knew and worshiped only Him? Where was Mother? Wouldn't we have known and worshiped Her also? Where was Her role honored?

What kind of a family is this?

Having graduated from Primary and Mutual, I've moved into Relief Society—the organization for women—and I've thought a lot about the feminine role as outlined by Mormon theology. Just what is it I have to look forward to as a Mormon woman?

If I obtain the ultimate Mormon glory, I will eternally give birth to spirit children who will populate new worlds that my husband/god will create. As an added incentive, I will eternally share this husband/god with His other wives. An eternal shortage of men.

My glory in this plan is my relationship with my children, but before they're born onto an earth, they will know and worship only their Father. And after they're born onto an earth, they will still pray to and worship only their Father. I won't communicate with them, and they won't be able to pray to me. I will be a gagged goddess.

Just where is the appeal here? Why did my pioneer foremothers sacrifice their all for a gospel that held such a bleak future for women? My ultimate "exaltation" sounds less like heaven and more like hell.

So I'm still wondering, and pondering, and praying. And I'm including Her in my prayers.

And while I'm sorting it all out, I admit it: I still enjoy playing with dolls. In fact, I have inherited many dolls from my mom's doll collection—antique Kewpie dolls with chubby cheeks, Oriental dolls with rich embroidered gowns, and Indian dolls with long dark braids.

But since I've grown up, I no longer associate my concept of deity with playing with dolls. I look beyond plastic and porcelain to find God. Being restricted to producing spirits eternally is as preposterous an idea as eternally playing with dolls.

There has to be more to being a goddess.

Although I have purchased many dolls for my daughters, I have also taught them that there's more to look forward to in the eternities than being impregnated by their husband/god and merely producing spirit children. Just as there is more to life than playing with dolls, there's more to eternity than producing spirit children.

Instead of a doctrine that defines a woman's eternal potential as a glorified womb, I seek a philosophy that illuminates the role of women and applauds the feminine half of humanity—one that encourages women everywhere to step up and seek all the splendacious opportunities the universe holds for growth, a philosophy that inspires women to reach jubilantly for the radiance of the stars.

The question in my heart is, how in the world is reaching for the stars in harmony with Mormon theology concerning women?

Would you like to swing on a star,
Carry moonbeams home in a jar,
Or would you like to just play with dolls
And be a Mormon woman after all?

(With thanks to Johnny Burke and Bing Crosby)

TWENTY-FIVE

BEWITCHED, BOTHERED, AND BEWILDERED IN ST. GEORGE
1999

I wish I could look at a clock and see the time, but there's no clock ticking on the wall. In fact, I can't see a clock anywhere. He even took my wrist-watch when I first came into his office. I must have been here more than an hour already, and my appointment was supposed to cost $150 for an hour and a half. I hope he won't charge me even more if we go over.

He nods, encouraging me to continue.

"I've studied the Church manuals, the scriptures, and prayed about all of them." I grab another tissue from the box on the table and sniff noisily. "But wherever I turn, everything just gets worse."

He prods for more information. "And then there's a whole other problem. I'd heard that the Church had rewritten part of its history, but I didn't believe it. I couldn't. Not *my* Church. I've read some of Professor Michael Quinn's works. You've heard of him, the Mormon historian who was also a history professor at BYU?"

His expression doesn't change, so I ask,

"He was named professor of the year?"

Getting no reaction, I go on.

"Anyway, he's documented some of those changes, but I refused to believe it. But then I saw it for myself in an old copy of the *Doctrine and Covenants*, guess it's a special edition or something, because it has an introduction and historical notes later ones don't have. . . It's a book my father gave me. . . . I read this quote in the footnotes, a promise by Joseph Smith to his wife Emma that he'd make 'more complete the organization of the Church by organizing the women in the order of the Priesthood.'" I stop to blow my nose again.

He says nothing.

"It's so powerful I memorized it to share in my Gospel Doctrine class. A week later, I saw another copy of the same old edition of the *Doctrine and Covenants* in a Mormon bookstore a few blocks from my home. . . . In fact, there were two copies there. . . . I checked them both."

My Kleenex tries without success to absorb the sound of another blow.

"They both had later publishing dates than 1941, like mine . . . and that quote I had found in my dad's copy . . . the one I memorized about Joseph Smith giving the priesthood to women? . . . had been taken out from the middle of the footnote. . . . And then I knew . . . *I knew* Michael Quinn was telling the truth . . . that the Church . . . *my Church* . . . really had changed their history . . . and deleted the part about giving the priesthood to women."

I look at his blurry image through my tears. "The Church did go back and *change things* in their history. It's there in black and white. I have the book."

What time is it?

Dr. Madison, who sits across from me in his sparsely-decorated office, was recommended by my friend Dianne back in Hesperia. His fleshy jaws are mere birthdays away from transforming into sagging jowls and tend to jiggle when his mouth moves, which hasn't occurred much so far. I've driven over four hours to meet with him here in Utah for a private session.

He specializes in helping clients release negative energy and claim positive, well-balanced energy in their lives. A well-respected member of the Mormon Church and in the community here in St. George, he also owns this clinic.

Up to this point I've done all the talking, crying, wiping, and blubbering. Now comes his turn, the moment I've waited for. His diagnosis is short and stinging.

"You're possessed by evil spirits."

I'm also stunned. "What?"

"I'm saying Satan holds power over you making you believe these lies."

"Why . . . why would you say such a thing?" I stammer.

"You've been taught the truth your entire life." His voice rises, almost angry. His jaw jiggles in agitation. "To turn away from it now as an adult can only be brought about by one thing, and that is the power of evil. Just like the homosexuals—you're possessed."

He pauses and runs his hand lightly through his thinning hair. "Plus, you've gone over the time allotted." He stands up, picks up my wristwatch and drops it into my hand. "You've been here more than two and a half hours, but instead of charging you $250 as I should, I'll only charge you $200."

Somewhere in a land too close to home, the gong of a medieval clock begins to strike thirteen, and minions and gargoyles gleefully shriek in collusion. A black crow spreads his wings, caws loudly, and flies toward an orange-crested moon.

Just yesteryear, I would have sworn it was impossible for such a medieval outrage to occur.

Just yesteryear, I would have sworn it was impossible for the Church to change its written history.

And just yesteryear, I would have sworn it was impossible that I'd ever be possessed to leave it.

TWENTY-SIX

MUTINY
1999

"om!"

My youngest daughter's voice blusters through my phone line, and the worrywart part of my momhood springs alive. Barely an hour has passed since I dropped her and two of her friends off at church for morning seminary, the scripture class held at oh dark thirty before high school. Mormon youth in every state in the United States and one hundred and forty countries around the globe attend these early morning classes.

I hurried home after taking her and pulled my Mercury wagon back into the garage just before the first day-care child arrived and rang my bell.

"Honey, what's wrong?" I ask, slowing the flow of Cheerios into small yellow bowls in front of my hungry charges.

"I just stomped out of seminary," I hear her say, sounding seriously ticked off. "And I'm *never* going back!"

I picture her mass of honey-gold curls shaking around her determined head as her uproar continues. Her hair has always been her crowning glory, ever since those first blonde ringlets appeared when she was a toddler. Little did I realize as I combed those baby curls, however, that they formed as naturally as would her growing inclination to be unswayed by anyone ever trying to tell her what to do.

Six small bodies fidget in front of me, waiting for their breakfast.

"Our whole lesson was on DOMA this morning, Mom. Nothing about scriptures at all," she continues.

DOMA, the California Defense of Marriage Act, which denied marriage between same-sex partners by defining marriage as exclusively the union of one man and one woman, has triggered hot debates in the courts. We will later learn that the Church had required Mormon seminary teachers all over California to give the gotta-vote-for-DOMA lesson that week.

Her voice rushes on through the phone in a rankled tone. "And my teacher said we should go home and tell our parents if they don't vote the way the Church says on DOMA, we won't make the Celestial Kingdom. Our whole family won't get to live with God!"

"*What?*" My breakfast preparations screech to a halt.

"I don't believe it, Mom. In fact, it's just wrong for them to tell us how to vote. I'm so mad, I left the class before I told them what I *really* think."

What she really thinks is that the Church should quit shoving a political issue down her apolitical throat. Church leaders have already bugged her to take part in a "youth service project" by placing "Yes on DOMA" signs in people's yards. No way is she getting roped into that.

And what I really think is that the ship of voting one's conscience should be a private vessel, not something to be shanghaied by plundering pirates shouting, "Vote as we say, swabbies, or instead of going to heaven, ye'll all walk the plank."

Gutsy, my daughter. She can easily justify her mutiny. Although there seem to be many things that my headstrong teen daughter and I disagree on these days, this, for sure, is not one of them.

Although the Church won't have much luck trying to hijack the mind of this particular young lady, such tactics work better with most other members.

When I first receive e-mails stating the Church is *assessing* each ward a specific amount to contribute to DOMA, I figure those danged anti-Mormons must be at work online spreading malicious lies about the Church. After all, there just isn't any way possible the Church would become so financially involved in a political election. That just wouldn't be right.

Would it?

Little did I know. Within a month, Brother Gaskins, who a short time later will become Bishop Gaskins, knocks briskly on my door. When I open it, he steps inside and shakes my hand, then gets right to the purpose of his visit.

"Sister, can the youth put a 'Yes on DOMA' sign in your yard?"

"No," I say, keeping it simple.

Here we go with those doggone signs again.

"The Church is really pushing this."

"I understand," I say, without inviting him to sit down.

He probably has no clue just how well I understand. With the help of the Internet, I even understand the Church's frustration that many of those plastic signs have been inexplicably delayed on their trip across the sea from China.

"No," I repeat again, as his rigid posture hasn't changed.

An awkward pause follows, especially since we're still standing in my entry hall. But after a bit of chitchat, I figure the time is now or never. Rather than asking *if* our ward has a dollar assessment, I hold my breath and innocently ask *the amount* of our ward's assessment.

He replies, "Three thousand dollars."

Damn. The rumors are true.

After he leaves, I realize it could have been much, much worse. Since our high desert area is less affluent than many other Southern California areas, our stake dodges the higher assessments, up to fifty thousand dollars, levied in wealthy stakes.

The Church's organization runs as smoothly as a slippery eel sliding through murky waters, deftly avoiding the legal seaweed complications that dangle all around.

The Church sends a letter to stake presidents, the local authorities overseeing wards and bishops, giving specific advice: "Experience shows that it is generally more successful to begin with the more affluent members, suggesting an appropriate contribution and thereafter extend the invitation to those of lesser means."

A widow friend of mine, whose granddaughter comes to my day care, goes right for her checkbook when the bishop comes campaigning at her door. He tells her to make her check out to DOMA instead of the Church, explains it isn't tax deductible, and gives her the mailing address. The part she isn't told is that her name and the amount of her contribution will be put on a list and sent to the stake president. This way, the leaders know who *has obeyed*, and, more importantly, who *has not obeyed*, Church counsel.

By assessing every California ward, huge amounts of money flow from Mormon members into the campaign coffers of DOMA, like they will for Proposition 8, which will succeed it in 2008. These shenanigans all catch the attention of Mark Leno, a San Francisco City Supervisor, who calls for an investigation on the tax-exempt status of the Church.

The next morning when I open my newspaper, I spot a letter to the editor written by a prominent Mormon couple in our ward. Their letter encourages local residents to vote yes on DOMA "to defend traditional marriage." This hypocrisy is over the top. I know "traditional marriage" doesn't run in their family, as they proudly claim polygamist ancestry. Polygamy might be many things, but "traditional" is *not* one of them.

Two days later the paper publishes another letter to the editor—mine, under an assumed name. If I were a braver woman, I'd sign my real name, but I'm not yet ready to reveal my true beliefs to my Mormon friends and face whatever consequences they might bring to my door.

The most succinct representation of the Church's historical hypocrisy is shown in a cartoon I find and stick on my fridge. It features Brigham Young, second prophet of the Mormon Church, with his more than fifty polygamous wives huddled behind him. In it, Brigham points an accusatory finger at two young cowboys holding hands, and cries, "But but but . . . that's not normal!"

My willful daughter finds an easy way to deal with these Church absurdities: she just never goes back—to seminary or to church. It isn't quite that simple for me, as I have lived my entire life in the seemingly safe Mormon port of Submit, Follow, and Obey, but in addition to struggling with the doctrines, I'm no longer finding refuge here.

I began to understand what mariners do when their vessel is overrun with scurrying rats or becomes hopelessly full of leaks—they abandon ship. But can I jump out alone, without first tightening a sure philosophy around me as a life and faith preserver?

TWENTY-SEVEN

FISHERS OF MEN
2000

*T*wo bicycles skid to a stop in our driveway.

"The missionaries are here, Mom. I'll get the door," my daughter eagerly volunteers as she spots them. Although the young elders in their distinctive dark pants, white shirts, and helmets had declined our invitation for a ride, they had accepted our invitation for dinner with hallelujah smiles.

"I'll turn off the TV," my other daughter says, running for the remote. She knows it's against mission rules for the missionaries to watch television, be on the Internet, or listen to the radio, and we don't want them to get in trouble.

Whenever the missionaries come through my front door, their enthusiasm sails in with them. This may have something to do with their anticipating three cute teenage girls sitting with them around the table. I know I'm bending the rules by inviting them into our all-female home, but I do it anyway. This is about as rule-bendy as I get, even though I don't have to worry, like the missionaries do, about a mission president who can kick me out.

"Come on in, elders," I welcome. These dedicated and eager young men are part of the fifty-thousand-plus-missionary proselytizing net the Church casts around the world to catch converts and share its gospel message.

As I shake hands with both missionaries, I can see the glint in their eyes that comes from believing they have special status because they belong to the "only true Church." I recognize this feeling within me with a pang of guilt, because I grew up feeling the same way.

The first question I ask each missionary is, "Where are you from, elders?"

"Utah!" or "Florida!" they reply, always with their ask-me-about-the-Church-and-I'll-dunk-you-in-the-water smiles.

As we share a Sunday roast and corn on the cob, I wonder how long it's been since I felt like they do, that my faith elevates me above those not so fortunate to have been born into a faithful Mormon family. It's hard to remember for sure, but it was long before years of living widened my understanding, long before Mormonism's promise of a forever family vanished before my eyes, and long before I began to suspect that some truths don't have to be dug out from a hill, but reside innately inside.

In the eyes of these young missionaries, everything in their whole Mormon cosmos will always line up exactly as God ordains. All they have to do is follow the rules handed them, and their lives will be just as golden as the plates Joseph Smith found in a New York hillside—if not in this life, then in the next. Golden-clad, guaranteed.

But what are my options here? Should I jump on the table atop the green Jell-O salad and shout, "Look up the Book of Abraham fiasco!" or stomp about over the mashed potatoes and yell, "Don't you know that Brigham Young taught that Adam was God?"

Hardly. I see no reason to douse the enthusiasm of these determined young men by pointing out complications in Church history or contradictions in doctrine, so we talk of other things.

Teaching Gospel Doctrine has changed me radically from an "eyes closed, I'm all in," kind of Mormon, to an "eyes open, trying to make changes" kind of Mormon. But am I making any headway in my class? Is it even possible to make changes? Mormonism may still be my heritage, but it no longer feels like home. Everyone around this table would be blown out of the water if I were to admit I've given up on the "truth" of Mormonism, but since I'm still teaching Gospel Doctrine, dinner is served.

We don't talk with the missionaries about their rules, either, because we already know they live under rules that cover every circumstance. According to the Missionary Handbook (pp. 20—35), they always travel in pairs of two, and they must

- sleep in the same room as their companion,
- stay within sight and hearing distance of their companion,
- protect their companion from porn,
- listen only to Church music,

- read only Church-approved books, and
- read only Church magazines.

They must not
- sleep in the same bed as their companion,
- ever be alone except when going to the bathroom,
- go swimming or take part in water sports (remember, "the waters are cursed"),
- keep score if they play basketball,
- go to movies, or
- write to the prophet.

And then, of course, they must strictly obey the biggest rule: Keep the opposite sex at arm's length at all times. Sexual sins are serious. Sometimes a missionary is sent home under suspicion of disgrace, leaving ward members speculating what sin he committed. Even a sin such as masturbation can be grounds to send an elder packing.

These elders who eat at our table have all passed the missionary-scrutinizing process. Strict rules govern who can or cannot serve a mission, as outlined in the Church Handbook of Instructions on pages 79-80.

Ineligible members include those who are HIV positive, or unworthy because of serious transgressions such as heavy petting, homosexual activity, or other sexual "perversions." Those members generally excluded include those who have submitted to, performed, encouraged, paid for, or even arranged for an abortion; members who have fathered or mothered a child out of wedlock; men under twenty-six and women under forty who have been divorced; and anyone who has participated in homosexual activity after age sixteen.

This Church Handbook of Instructions is not available to the general membership of the church, only to bishops and top leaders, which explains why I'd never heard of these particular rules. In fact, it is in violation of Church policy for members to have a copy of any of these rules. Imagine displaying right out in front of everyone the rules that can get a member in trouble!

In 1999, however, the Utah Lighthouse Ministry published a portion of the Handbook on the Internet to help individuals remove their names from the Church, which resulted in a huge scuffle with the legal system of the Church. Think Church lawyers showing up at the door of the ministry.

According to the Lighthouse website, www.utlm.org:

The irony in all this is that by the very fact of making a legal issue about posting parts of the *Handbook*, the LDS Church made the general public aware that there was a secret handbook regulating church disciplinary action. This led to people all over the world searching on the Internet for copies. Their legal action amounted to blowing feathers in the wind and never being able to retrieve them.

Another point of irony is that the international attention given the lawsuit helped quadruple the number of people coming to our web site.

The Utah Lighthouse Ministry removed their URL's until the case against them was, of course, ultimately dismissed. But in the meantime the Salt Lake Tribune printed a newspaper article about the ruckus, thus spreading the availability of the Church Handbook of Instructions on the forbidden tree of Internet sites. This is how I obtained the quotes I refer to above about missionary worthiness, because this information would never have come from my bishop.

The missionaries pitch in to help suds up our wood-paneled station wagon and cover themselves with flour while punching down pizza dough, and Elder Erickson even gives us the inspiration for the name of our cutest puppy, Eric. We squelch a giggle when we tell him, though, because Eric is a girl.

One Saturday afternoon after working in the yard all morning free from day-care kiddies, I'm taking a break, arranging some freshly cut peach iris. My middle daughter comes in panting, wearing her running shorts. She grabs a cup of cold water, gulps it down, and leans up against the kitchen counter.

"Great track practice today, Mom. We ran all the way to the freeway and back." Her hair is scrunched back in a ponytail, and sweat glistens on her face. She rarely bothers with makeup because she just doesn't need it. Even after a strenuous run, with her looks, all she needs to add to that face is a smile. The guys never have a chance.

"Dang—good job! That's what . . . five miles each way?" I ask as I finish scooping up blossom-laden stalks and coaxing them into an arrangement.

"Even further, I think." The tap water sloshes around the green stalks as it fills the vase. She waits, watching the water spill over the side until I shut off the tap, then adds, "There's something I want to talk about."

I set the vase down and turn to face her.

"I've thought a lot about it." She picks up an iris stalk and strokes the soft fuzz of its petals. "If I go on a mission, would you help pay for it?"

"Of course I will, honey."

Her question doesn't surprise me. After all, she grew up singing, "I Hope They Call Me on a Mission" in Primary and often talks about joining the Peace Corps when she gets older. The Church would be luckier than blue blazes to get this gal to knock on doors for them.

I give her a hug, pull out two kitchen chairs, and try to remember when it happened that this young woman replaced my little girl in Strawberry Shortcake jammies. Even though I've lost all confidence that I can find shiny truth in Mormonism, she still wants to serve. She exudes self-confidence that she can get whatever she wants out of life. I can't help but wonder how different my life might have been if I had possessed such assurance at her age.

"This is my plan," she continues. "I'll work, save my money, and pay half. Since I can't go until I'm twenty-one anyway, I have three years. Plenty of time. Then, would you pay a fourth?" She quickly adds, "And I'll ask Dad if he'll pay a fourth, too."

"If this is what you really want, I'll support you wholeheartedly." I squeeze her hand. "Where better to spend my hard-earned money than on you?"

Besides, I know she'll work hard and save harder, as this isn't just small change we're talking about. A mission costs $400 a month or $7,200 for the eighteen months. If she were male, she'd serve twenty-four months, and the cost would run $9,600. Volunteer work can get expensive.

Missions for girls are shorter so they can get home and dive back into the pool of eligible marriage partners sooner.

"Just think, Mom, I'll get to help others and share the truth. I know I can't choose where they send me, but I've always wanted to travel the world. And wouldn't it just be so cool if they do send me someplace exotic?"

I'm sure all missionaries share the fantasy of being sent to exciting ports all over the world—Paris, Madrid, Hong Kong, or those other "faraway places with the strange-sounding names" my dad used to sing about. And, yes, some missionaries are actually sent to far-off lands. But most are sent to less glamorous spots, like member-saturated Utah, the flat farmlands of the Midwest, or desert communities like ours. Wherever they're called, however, they always claim with pride, "It was the best mission in the whole world."

But sometimes the wind just blows the wrong way. At the next General Conference, the prophet speaks again on preparing our youth to go on a mission, and although the message isn't new, there's an added emphasis on the proper gender for the missionary force.

"Young men must prepare to serve a mission," he admonishes. "Young women, on the other hand, must prepare for marriage."

The next week in Sunday school, the boys in my daughter's class razz her about her missionary dreams. "Didn't you hear what the prophet said last week? *Boys* go on a mission. Not *girls*."

My daughter fumes. What a can of worms.

She's determined to smash that missionary-glass ceiling, but her enchantment for missionary service wanes at the same rate that her disillusionment grows. Girls can't serve until they're twenty-one so they won't miss any marriage proposals, and she's just eighteen. Although the age requirements will drop in 2012 to nineteen for girls and eighteen for boys, that's too far away to influence her decision. During the next three years, she'll enter a nursing program, spend a semester in Spain, travel to Russia to teach children English, and fall madly in love—with traveling. Her original missionary motivation will blossom instead into a love of partaking of other cultures all over the globe. Marriage will still show up soon enough.

Back in 1966, my brother received his mission call to New Zealand. It sounded like a pretty exotic place to go, with its far-flung outlying islands, long marine-filled coastline, those funny kiwi birds, and most importantly, people just waiting for the message he would bring.

Paying for his mission was a huge sacrifice for my family, but one that had been planned for since the day the doctor said, "It's a boy!" The announcement, "It's a girl!" doesn't bring the same automatic thought process. Mormon boys start saving early by pushing pennies into their missionary piggy banks. Members also believe the Lord showers financial blessings on a family while their missionary serves.

My folks watched patiently for these blessings.

"While Jason is on his mission," my cousin Linnet told my parents, "you know I won't take a penny for Lorelei's piano lessons. It's my small contribution."

Mom beamed and readied her umbrella for the continuing downpour. Free piano lessons did help, but that was where the downpour ended.

Although Mom felt conflicted going against the Church's stance on working outside the home, our family had a missionary to support, so she put her umbrella back in the rack and went to work. Fortunately, her creativity and outgoing personality landed her a job at the Paris Company Department Store, where she demonstrated embroidery on White sewing machines.

At my brother's missionary farewell, a Sunday service where soon-to-be missionaries speak and receive congratulations from ward members, one of my mom's friends, a plump lady wearing a typical Mormon floral figure-concealing dress, placed her hand on my shoulder and asked, "Won't you miss your brother while he's gone for two whole years?"

Honestly, as I looked back into her questioning eyes, I didn't know how to answer her. Of course I loved my brother, but why should I miss him when he was off doing what God wanted him to do, and what he'd wanted to do since he was old enough to know what it was he wanted to do?

My brother served a two-year mission. Of course I didn't, because I was a girl. And apparently, things hadn't changed that much thirty years later when my daughter wanted to go on a mission. She didn't go, either, because she had to wait three years, because she's a girl.

A Canadian man I date has a daughter who works for the Church headquarters in a distinctive capacity: arranging passage home for the bodies of deceased missionaries. With a missionary force of more than fifty thousand, tragedies happen. Accidents, murders, suicides. There's a funeral in my home ward for a missionary who died by suicide. After he struggled with depression on the other side of the world, this young man threw himself in front of a bus.

Signs of mental illness often appear in the late teens or early adult years, and these nineteen-year-old kids can be far away from home.

Mormons believe missionary service will be the great work of the spirit world after this life, as all of God's children must have the opportunity to accept the truth of Mormonism. No lying around on clouds, playing gold harps in the Mormon Heaven, as there will still be real missionary work to be done on the other side.

Mormon elders take seriously the exhortation to be "fishers of men" and share the beliefs of Mormonism. Their tackle-box tools include sharing the Book of Mormon, bearing their testimony, and grinning big happy smiles. The proof they offer potential converts is to pray and "feel the spirit" about their message. The Church believes having Mormon missionaries in every country is one of the "signs of the times." Even the second coming of Jesus Christ will be postponed until every nation receives the Mormon missionaries.

Their efforts cover the globe, from small towns in Utah to the Down Under of Australia. These young missionaries remain committed, although convert baptism rates have been slowing and converts are leaving the Church in record numbers.

Although I might not be much of a believer in fate, an outside force as strong as the moon's gravitational pull on all the fish in the sea is about to rip me out of the Mormon net surrounding me and wash me up on a whole new sandy shore.

TWENTY-EIGHT

KISSING THE SAILS OF SHIPS
2000

*S*hips sometimes go *smash* in the night, and my ship of teaching Gospel Doctrine just *smashed* into the rocky cliff, ending that voyage. I'm released from teaching the class.

I've taught for almost four years, longer than many teachers have, and I admit it hasn't been without waves of controversy. I've been walking two planks of conscience and scripture for a long time. I've based my lessons on the scriptures, not the manual, which has led to several heated discussions in class, as well as several conversations with Bishop Zone.

When I talked to him about an issue the manual insisted I teach, which I pointed out was fish-stinking wrong, he simply asked me, "So what are you going to do?"

I replied, "I won't teach it. Besides, no one will know I'm leaving it out."

Another week, a new convert unfamiliar with the Mormon concept of multiple gods got so upset when I mentioned the belief that he streaked out of class and raced right into the bishop's office to howl his complaints. After all, if every worthy male can become a god, it stands to reason there are lots of gods out there. The next week, my bishop strode into my class and announced, "We're lucky to have a teacher so knowledgeable about the gospel."

But standing in front of this class each Sunday hasn't been easy. Although my bishop has supported me, Brother Dickenson, the Sunday school superintendent, for whatever reason, from the day he was called to the position last year announced his intention to get me released. He finally got his way. Oh, the hazards of being a single woman trying to widen people's perspectives in a male-dominated church.

I've tried to make a difference. I've come to believe that the way change takes place is from the inside, and each Sunday, my goal has been to make some small changes in the way people view things. It feels good—powerful, even—to attempt this.

A woman I barely know tells me, "I've always loved your classes because you make me look at things in different ways." That's been my whole idea.

Although I'll miss teaching and all the things I learn every week, my dolphin friends Reason and Logic have been gasping for fresh air long enough. But since now I won't have to be there for my class each Sunday, I'll make the break clean and ask to be released from my additional callings of playing the organ in Sunday school and being a counselor in the young woman's organization.

My Sundays are now adrift.

I've had a foot on two different shorelines for some time, with the shores drifting farther and farther apart. The inevitable has happened—I've studied my way out of Mormonism. I know I can never go back.

So now where can I find Truth? Is Truth a granite-hard entity? Or instead, does it float as a light vapor over the sea, in soft mists, kissing the sails of ships? If so, how do I catch, tame, and verify such a misty fog? And what can I tell my daughters? Should we just join hands and run wild through valley and vale chasing Truth through all four corners of this round earth? Or will Truth come softly to us, unannounced and unexpected, one spring morning, or one winter afternoon?

TWENTY-NINE

FISHING AROUND
2001

A shining ball of light ball of light and love named Reverend Mary is introduced to me by a silver-haired man I meet at the Diamond Ballroom in Redlands. I begin driving the hundred-mile round trip to Riverside each Sunday morning to be part of her congregation. Imagine, a woman, a beautiful black woman, preaching from the pulpit.

This congregation dynamically blends black and white faces. After I have spent fifty years in an all-white church, attending this church stretches my former world of color and gender into new shapes.

Although some blacks have joined the Mormon Church since the policy change in 1978, most of the new members don't know about the previous prophetic statements against their race. There is only one black member in my old ward whom the missionaries had tracked out and baptized, a dynamite gal named Rachael whose no-nonsense-don't-mess-with-me personality adds a new dimension of pizzazz to the Mormon community. One day I had braved the question and asked her if she believed God is really a *white man.*

She laughed good-naturedly and said, "Of course not."

Dumbfounded, I asked, "Then . . . why did you join the Mormon Church?"

She answered simply, "I just overlook that part."

My guess is she'll find more and more parts to overlook.

When Rachael was called to teach seminary, the early morning class for high school students and a required class to attend BYU, I heard via the gossip line that another member complained to the stake president.

"She shouldn't be in that position," he had arrogantly affirmed, "because of the curse."

I doubt if she read any of the quotes from the early Church leaders, including prophets, but obviously most of the older members have—quotes such as this one:

> Not only was Cain called upon to suffer [for killing Abel], but because of his wickedness he became the father of an inferior race. A curse was placed upon him and that curse has been continued through his lineage and must do so while time endures. Moreover, they have been made to feel their inferiority and have been separated from the rest of mankind from the beginning. Enoch saw the people of Canaan, descendants of Cain, and he says, "and there was a blackness came upon all the children of Canaan, that they were despised among all people." . . . In the spirit of sympathy, mercy and faith, we will also hope that blessings may eventually be given to our negro [sic] brethren, for they are our brethren—children of God—notwithstanding their black covering emblematical of eternal darkness. (Joseph Fielding Smith [later the tenth prophet], *The Way to Perfection,* 1935, pp. 101-102)

I find the last words of this quote most chilling. Some things just take years, and years, and tears, to wash away.

Although Rachael might have accepted at least most of Mormonism's doctrine, she struggled with the music. As she put it, "Mormon music is too la-de-da-de-da." She even confessed to me she sometimes goes back to her old Baptist church to get a shot in the arm of "real gospel music."

Once I hear the music erupting all around the stained glass windows in the church in Riverside, I know what Rachael's been talking about. When their choir comes marching in, all happiness breaks loose. Swelling with the joy of being alive, their music shouts out themes of validation and love.

This Sunday morning, the woman offering the opening prayer entreats, "We pray for those of us worshiping in this church service, and we pray for those not here, who are enjoying their boats on a lake. We pray for them . . ."

At this, my Mormon script kicks right in to finish the thought "to see the light, repent of their sinful ways, and be here in church with us next week." But instead, I hear ". . . and give thanks for them, too, knowing they are right where they should be this day, enjoying the beauties of nature."

Right where they should be, enjoying a day on a lake with their family on Sunday? You mean people should seek to enjoy their lives?

Maybe the framers of the Declaration of Independence were onto something when they said our Creator endowed all men with the rights of "Life, Liberty and the pursuit of Happiness."

Could my most lofty purpose—instead of enduring to the end—be to pursue happiness and experience joy?

On Easter Sunday, I arrive early to get a front-row seat. The choir is on fire, and at the end of Reverend Mary's sermon, I wipe away the tears that stream down my cheeks. After the closing song, I almost fall off the pew when who hops down the aisle but a six-foot Easter bunny! Since I'm sitting on the front row, my eyes fly to Reverend Mary, who turns toward my shocked face and explains, "Why not? He's as real as anything else."

Each Monday evening, I drive another hundred-mile round trip to attend a Bible class that Reverend Mary teaches. After all, if the Mormons don't have it right, who does? Truth must pop its shiny face up someplace. As soon as the last day-care child is picked up, I jump in my car and head down the mountain pass. I arrive home when the time is pushing heavily against eleven o'clock.

At the end of the three-month class, we're assigned a project to share what we've learned. I finish writing what I feel is quite a remarkable summary of my fifty-year Mormon background, which leads me to continue seeking truth with Reverend Mary.

I share this with my friend Ken, who was my chiropractor until we started dating, and expect to hear words of hearty appreciation. Instead he says, "You must write a song to go with it!"

"Who, me?" I protest. "I don't write songs."

"Then I'll write it for you."

"But, but, what about the music?" I bluster. "I happen to know writing music is a big deal!"

"That's not a problem," he insists. "I'll just put it to music everyone already knows."

It takes a lot of push and shove for him to convince me, because after all, *he* isn't the one with the mediocre alto voice who will have to sing in front of people, but he finally talks me into it. After I gather my courage, I present it the next Monday evening to our small Bible class in Riverside, song and all. But I'm in for a total surprise when Reverend Mary tells me she wants the entire congregation to hear it!

The very next Sunday morning, with a congregation of over three hundred people in front of me and one of the most incredible choirs in Southern California behind me, I stand at the podium holding a microphone. I'm bolstered with the support of my youngest daughter, the only one now at home, and two Mormon girlfriends who have made the drive with us, smiling up at me from the congregation. After I read my-oh-so-lofty written presentation, the organist begins his glorious introduction—including foot pedals—and as I try to calm my quivering voice, I begin. The congregation joins in with me on each chorus, the adrenaline kicks in, and zing, what a feeling!

DRIVE ON

(Tune: Battle Hymn of the Republic)

"Seeking God's a pain," I think as I get in my car.
A hundred-mile round trip to church is really much too far.
But it's a tiny price to pay for following my star,
And so I just drive on.

Chorus
Glory, Glory Hallelujah
Now I really want to clue ya
Reverend Mary socks it to ya
I know I must drive on!

I know my old religion stands for lots of things that grate.
Women, Indians, blacks, and gays all are second rate.
Deep inside I know this stuff can never be my fate.
And so I just drive on.

(Chorus)

My Mormon kinsmen sang a song eight-score years ago,
When they left their homes in Illinois and trudged off through the snow.
They walked to Utah for their faith a thousand miles or so.
Their hymn was called "Drive On."

(Chorus)

I'm still on that journey started many years before.
Like them, my life has changed, and now I'm seeking something more.
If I don't find dem pearly gates, at least I will explore.
I know I must drive on.

The last stanza of Ken's song shines as a beacon in my life right now. I am seeking more, I will explore, and I'm sailing on.

THIRTY

JACUZZI MERMAID
2001

*A*h, the joy of bubble baths. The slippery bubbles sliding across my toes, the warm water swirling around my thighs, well, there's just something magical that happens when bubbles fill a tub. And there's just no better place in the whole universe to contemplate the purpose of life or the nature of truth, or to simply relax after a long day of caring for children.

I admit it, I'm an addict, ever since childhood. So when I see a Home Depot ad showing how a Jacuzzi tub could "easily replace" a regular tub, my inner mermaid is hooked.

My Jacuzzi project—because as my girls say, "Mom always needs a project"—starts out as a simple remodeling job to my small master bath. I'll just remove the shower and vanity, bump out an exterior wall, and add the jetted marvel. Paul the Wonder Contractor, hired from his newspaper ad, agrees he can complete my project within a couple of months.

But the Jacuzzi dream soon takes on a life of its own, taking us down a winding remodeling road neither one of us anticipates. I don't plan on adding a sitting room, fireplace, or walk-in closet. And I have no intention of quadrupling the size of the old bathroom under vaulted ceilings. Nevertheless, that's how the project evolves.

I also don't count on Paul's "slight" drinking problem causing countless delays and extensions. Since we start in January, it should be finished by Easter—my Easter basket! Well, no. Okay, by the Fourth of July—my firecracker! Doesn't happen. For sure by Thanksgiving—I'll be thankful. Nope, just a turkey. Christmas—a present? No star on that tree. But if we talk about eighteen long months later—now we're into the reality show called remodeling.

But when Paul finally sets the Jacuzzi tub, it's amidst a sea of glorious crema marfil marble and flanked against huge sections of glass block windows. It's more gorgeous than I could have dreamed.

One spring morning my doorbell rings, and a Church friend I haven't seen since my churchgoing days stands on my porch. Thelma's hoping, no doubt, to bring me back into the fold. Although in the past I had many Mormon friends, these days, such a visit is as rare as oyster teeth. Eagerly, I share my triumph with her.

"Oh—those windows!" she cries as her eyes scan the glass blocks behind the Jacuzzi tub, and she strokes the marble countertops. Then she peers over her bifocals at the oversized glass-block and marble shower, and her eyes hesitate on the two showerheads. A puzzled look crosses her face which softens into a conclusion as she says, "Oh, I see . . . so you can get your front and back wet at the same time."

"That must be it, Thelma," I say, smiling and not explaining further.

A week later, another friend stands on my front porch for the official "tour of the retreat." One of my few non-Mormon friends, Tonya moved from Samoa to marry a man who lives nearby. She prances into the retreat with oohs and aahs and then catches sight of the two showerheads gleaming in bronze decadence in the same opulent shower. She cups her hands in front of her mouth and whispers to me knowingly, "You need a friend."

A salty old sea-faring captain couldn't better explain the differences between Mormons and mermaids. Besides, she's right on—a friend is *exactly* what I need.

THIRTY-ONE

BAILING
2002

*P*aul Simon may know fifty ways to leave your lover, but leaving the Mormon Church isn't quite so easy. Most who leave simply drift away. A more difficult route is resigning your membership through a complicated process of hoop-jumping the Church calls "name removal." In past years, many members who tried to resign found themselves summoned to a hastily assembled Church court—and excommunicated.

Should I lounge in the sailboat of drifting away or actively man the battleship and resign my membership?

So far, all of my decisions about the Mormon Church have been hinged on doctrine, and this ends up being no exception. It ties back to Joseph Smith and the problem of him saying God was a spirit, after his First Vision experience when he claimed to see God's body. When I had asked my bishop, he couldn't explain it, but some time later, I stumbled upon the answer.

It's simple—Joseph Smith never claimed he saw Jesus and God. He said he saw "two personages." If Joseph *had* claimed those personages were deities, early Church leaders, his mother, and his brother should have known about it. Instead, we find these kinds of quotes regarding Joseph's First Vision.

Orson Hyde, an original member of the Quorum of the Twelve Apostles, said,

> Someone may say, "If this work of the last days be true, why did not the Savior come himself to communicate

this intelligence to the world?" Because to the angels was committed the power of reaping the earth, and it was committed to none else. (*Journal of Discourses*, 1854, Vol. 6, p. 335)

Second Mormon Prophet Brigham Young said, "The Lord did not come with the armies of heaven . . . But He did send His angel . . . " (*Journal of Discourses*, 1855, Vol. 2, p. 171)

Fourth Mormon Prophet Wilford Woodruff said the Church was established "by the ministering of an holy angel from God." (*Journal of Discourses*, 1855, Vol. 2, p. 196)

Even Joseph Smith's mother, Lucy Mack Smith, and his brother William Smith, both said it was "an angel" who appeared to Joseph in his vision.

Such doctrinal thunderbolts hardly faze me anymore, but I remember my question to my former bishop and wonder if I should share what I learned. Will he want to know the answer? The truth?

I ask my close friend Desiree what she thinks about my writing a friendly letter to him explaining the facts. I respect my friend's opinion. We both worked together in several Church organizations, and she's one of the bravest women I know. She's turning fifty, and her love is climbing steep cliffs of sheer rock, regardless of the height. She keeps her eyes focused above to the next hand hold and, as she explains it, "I just never look down."

Her quick reaction to my question doesn't sound quite so brave. In fact, it takes me off guard.

"Better think about that," she says.

"Why?" I ask.

"Because if they want to, they can hold a court and excommunicate you."

"For writing a letter?" I ask. "He's not even my bishop anymore. Come on."

"You could be accused of spreading false doctrine or being an apostate," she reminds me. "Punishable by excommunication."

I know she's right, as teaching "false doctrine" is right up there with all those sexual sins as reasons to get thrown out of the Church.

If I share what I've learned about Church history, it's possible I could trigger a court and be excommunicated. Although I don't give a minnow's fin about the status of my membership, to my Mormon friends, the word *excommunication* carries the stench of shame. Before I write a letter to my former bishop that takes this risk, I'd better first batten down the hatches and remove my name from Church records. This will make it aquamarine-clear I've left the Church *on my own terms.*

Many who leave the Church deal with heavy repercussions from family and friends, but my parents are both gone, and I feel their support in my heart. Even my closest friends have left the church for different, and substantial, reasons. That's one of the beauties of the Mormon Church—there are so many different reasons to leave.

Fortunately, I can go online and find details on the process to resign. Step one is to write my exit letter to the Church, documenting my request and stating my reasons. After much soul searching, I finish my eight-page letter on July 24, 2002.

July 24—a big day for Mormons, commemorating the day Brigham Young led the pioneers into the Salt Lake Valley to start a new life.

July 24—a big day in my life, commemorating the day I write to the Mormon Church and ask for my name to be removed. The day I start my new life.

I send my letter to the present bishop of my ward, Bishop Gaskins, the same man who came to my house asking if the youth could put DOMA signs in my yard. Weeks go by and I hear nothing. Since there is a whole department in Salt Lake Church headquarters designed just to handle requests from members wanting out, I call. I speak with a gentleman who calls my stake president, who presides over my bishop. I wondered if my bishop would ever call me to try and answer my questions or intervene, but he didn't.

I wait some more. And make another call to Salt Lake.

September comes. September goes.

On October 3 when I open my mailbox, I find a form letter from Bishop Gaskins saying my membership will be taken off in another *thirty days* unless I "rescind my request." Another thirty days? It has already been more than two months.

My bishop's letter clarifies that along with rescinding my membership, I will be rescinding Church blessings. Like the "blessing" of not counting. The "blessing" of being less than. The "blessing" of not being in heaven with the husband who left me for another woman. The "blessing" of being told to have faith and quit thinking so much. Got it. Toss them all overboard.

I'll take care of this. As soon as the last day-care child is picked up, I send a fax to Salt Lake and insist they remove my name without further delay. I thank the kind gentleman I had spoken with for his help, and I include a copy of the letter of postponement I received. I add an extra nudge and say I'm sure he can handle this without my obtaining legal representation.

My phone rings first thing the next morning. Good news! My request has at last been honored, and my name will be removed from the Church records—today.

The date is October 4.

Ten four. Over and out!

Stillness. I move away from the howling storm into a state of peaceful free fall. I'm unfettered as the wide-open sea. I leave behind the fray of disappointment, the commotion of ritual, and the frustration of colliding thoughts.

Tears. I shed tears for leaving the faith I've grown up with. Cleansing tears. Reforming tears. I shed tears on both sides of October 4, but with these new tears come calmness.

And peace. Peace with being . . . me.

THIRTY-TWO

WIDE-OPEN SEAS
2002

*T*he house has fallen quiet. I slide my arms up and down over the smooth sheets. It's only been a few weeks now that I've been indulging in this glorious freedom of enjoying the feel of bare skin on sheets.

Removing my garments felt like taking a deep breath, leaping off a high cliff, and plunging into deep waters. For years, I've lived a lifestyle that demanded I keep most of my body covered day and night. After all, the responsibility for any sexual sin, even rape, sits squarely on the woman for dressing immodestly. Spotting a sexy kneecap or upper arm of a woman could drive a man's desires beyond his capability to control. Garments do more than remind Mormons of Temple promises: they cover such tempting flesh.

But the time has come for me to emerge from my garment cocoon. Next week, I may even wear shorts in public during this summer heat wave. Years will pass before I'll dare to wear tank tops, as tentacles of control are hard to break.

For now, I revel in the satisfaction of sleeping *au natural*. I spread my arms across the width of my bed and kick my legs back and forth to fully luxuriate in this newfound pleasure. I'll never sleep in a nightgown again.

I haven't shared this particular change of dress code with any of my daughters. One's still in high school, one goes to the local college, and my oldest attends Utah State University.

The whirring fan above the bed pulls the summer night's air around the room in a soothing motion. I kick off the covers and savor the sensual feeling of the soft sheets underneath me while allowing the whisper of cool air to touch my bare skin from above.

Without warning, my bedroom door bursts open and my youngest daughter flips the switch, instantly flooding the room with light. Before I can pull a blanket across me, or she can say whatever she came to say, the sight before her stops her cold.

She turns and streaks from my room down the hallway, shouting the scandalous news to her sister—"Mom's not wearing her garments!"

I'm going to pull a Joseph Smith and start my own church, and I need a name with a star-rated kind of flair. Got it—**C.O.S.M.O.S**.

And it stands for, of course, Church Of Sleeping More On Sunday.

Summertime. The grass radiates out around me, and my flowers are blooming their heads off in a riot of summer color. It's their turn to show off and my turn to take it easy. I'll lie back on the lush grass I've just mowed and bask in the results of all my efforts.

Look at those soft fluffy clouds floating above me in the sky. All those funny mischievous shapes they're twisting themselves into. I don't often take the time to think about things in such a soft way. Instead, I'm used to viewing life in a hard way, with firm lines around everything. But lying on the summer grass of my yard, I'm doing just that, because so much has softened.

I've always worried about staying within the lines. Those solid, black, masculine lines drawn around me. I didn't ever consider if they were valid or ask if they were valid for me. I didn't consider moving those lines. I just didn't want to cross them.

Now, I realize the lines of decisions are up to me. I realize the importance of being responsible and observing the lines of consequences. That's the way to make my decisions. When I consider the consequences, I can draw my own lines.

I gaze up at the soft clouds floating overhead. Yep, that's the way I want to live—drawing my own lines.

THIRTY-THREE

WET
2003

I'm wet.

It's quite a concept, when I think of it, how a little moisture can change everything. Change the effect of a glance, change the aroma in a room, or change a kiss from something merely pleasant into a torrent of passion.

He wraps his strong arms tightly around my waist and pulls me toward him as we lie entwined in the sheets on his rumpled bed. His gentle hands explore my body, and any lingering thoughts I have of the day fade into mists of passion. The wetness grows and begins to surround us as our bodies melt into a churning current. We become one in a river's engulfing wave of passion as bubbles burst all around us. Our energy is changing, growing, swelling. I'm alive with this river. Outrageous and alive, as never before.

Rapids lie ahead. Unexpectedly, the waves surge in powerful bursts over the large rocks now emerging, crashing hard against the granite boulders, and spraying us with its hazy mist. The river rushes on with exhilarating urgency.

Then without warning, the energy of the water surrounding us subsides, and the river becomes tranquil, pausing in its downward journey to bend around the curving river's edge. The calmness envelopes us and offers a restful change of pace as we cling together and float effortlessly in the placid water.

Then, just as quickly as it subsided, the pulse of the current begins to accelerate. A roar from downstream warns us of what lies ahead—something more powerful, more magnificent and treacherous than even the rapids behind us. I'm filled with anticipation of the Niagara soon to come.

The river's strength blasts over us, holding us powerless against its fury, waiting to drown us in the liquid ecstasy. Even as those solid boulders appear in plain sight, I'm helpless to stop our forward motion and feverishly anticipate cascading over the rocky ledge. The river crashes around me with a deafening impact, sending white foam skyward as our torrent of passion continues, pulsating relentlessly toward the inevitable plunge ahead.

I'm drenched. Quivering at the precipice. A scream tears free from deep inside as anticipation overtakes me and a tremendous burst of fervor plunges me forward, plummeting us over the cascading falls, then downward, downward, downward, encased in ecstasy, as sprays of total energy and frothy white mist surrounds us.

Tranquility

and stillness

settle softly over us.

Then slowly, very slowly, I begin to breathe again.

"Wow," I whisper as the waves lap me back into reality. "That was incredible."

He whispers back, "I'm glad."

Breathless on a new unexpected shoreline, I'm washed free of old inhibitions that have clung to me as tightly as barnacles on a ship's hull. Now a new world of accountability has broken wide open for me, and I realize that decisions about my life, my body, and my relationships, are totally up to me. My answers lie inside myself. I should have figured this out years ago.

THIRTY FOUR

SAFE HARBOR
2004

*H*arbor lights on full alert. Sirens blare. Send out the Coast Guard. I'm six hundred miles from home, never been here before, and I'm by myself. The place is packed with unknowns and strangers. And look at that man—stars almighty, would you look at that man! And he's heading straight toward me.

Please, please, whatever gods there be, let that man be heading straight toward me.

My hands tremble. The music pulses. I barely remember why I'm here. Some foggy recollection of driving to Utah to attend my gorgeous sister's third wedding which will take place tomorrow. But all that exists tonight is this dance, and this man, who's now right in front of me.

"Like to dance?"

Our bodies are close together. We move rhythmically in each other's arms. Music must be playing over our heads, other couples must be swirling on the dance floor, and the moon must still be hanging high in the night sky. I couldn't tell you. All I know for sure is I'm dancing, and his name is James.

Danger lurks. Even though I'm not the shy girl I used to be, I still get uneasy around men. Why? Because deep down, I know I like men. And that's not a good thing, now is it? Can anything good possibly come from liking men? Or more to the point, from liking this gorgeous hunk of a charming, amazingly tall, incredible man?

Thank my lucky starfish, we do have things in common to talk about. He's also a Mormon, or used to be. He left the Church after his mission when he discovered major doctrinal problems in Church history. Sounds familiar. We talk long into the sunrise. Then the clouds part and he asks me *the* question: "Can I have your e-mail address?"

Although we live three states apart and we're both too rooted to our individual states and families for either of us to move, there's magic in the air. I know this won't last forever, but for however long it lasts, I'll take.

He drives to California, and we hike around Big Bear Lake. Later, we go white water rafting at Jackson Hole, Wyoming; see Siegfried and Roy in Las Vegas; trek up to the Emerald Pools in Zion National Park, and explore the ruins of Chichen Itza in Cancun. Really, we fly to Cancun. A fantasy trip of a lifetime with a man like James? Yes, it's true, all right. I'm the luckiest girl in the galaxy. Dream on, all you bikini-clad babes on the beach—he's with me. And I have the pictures to prove it.

Ah, the pictures. Those magical, sensual, life-affirming pictures James takes. Up until now, I've never felt sure of myself in front of a camera. My sister is the photogenic one, after all, not me. But in the pictures James take— and he likes to take pictures—I confidently smile back from the steps of an ancient pyramid, the columned arcades, and the turquoise waves of the Caribbean Sea. I shed my old self-doubts and wear a new kind of feeling good about myself.

As it turns out, men aren't necessarily so mystifying and dangerous after all. It's taken me over fifty years to figure out that appreciating our differences can make life just that much more fun. Call off the Coast Guard; I'm heading toward safe harbor. With a smile.

THIRTY-FIVE

THE MULTIFACETED BEAUTY
OF A CORAL REEF
2005

*T*he World Wide Web laces the entire world together. Although the Church initially champions this invention as being inspired by God to increase the pace of Mormon genealogy, it doesn't take long for the Church counsel to shift against using the Net because of its lurking danger of porn addiction.

But I find the Net has bigger fish to try—like dating sites.

There *are* Plenty of Fish in the sea, as the dating site with that name proudly advertises. After I conquer my initial hesitation, I discover that even for a woman in her fifties, this net holds men who like to dance, like to hike, like nice restaurants, like to cook, like geocaching, like movies, like musicals, like kayaking, like day trips, and like to have great conversations late into the night. It would be nice if I could combine all the qualities I admire into one ideal man, but even the powerful Internet doesn't guarantee a perfect match.

Then, after all the great dates, as well as all the grim dates, it's finally happened—I'm in love. A love shining with all the wild hues found in a tropical coral reef. Those aquamarine waters have nothing over this guy—he's all I've ever dreamed of. He also used to be Mormon, which gives us an added depth of connection because we've both loved and lost our whole belief system. It gives us a whole other language in which to communicate.

Although it's early October, the Christmas carols are starting to sing out overhead in the mall as we stroll hand in hand. Our magical love is beginning just as the most magical time of the year begins. As each carol floats around us in the air, I think, *This will be the best Christmas and most spectacular New Year's Eve of my life.*

"What did we do with our lives," I ask him, "before we met?"

"We looked for each other," he answers with a kiss.

But by Christmastime, the magic has dissipated into the stratosphere and I'm not able to fly fast enough to catch it. My heartbreak will keep Cupid and me in a standoff for years to come.

But on New Year's Eve, would anyone on that dance floor ever guess that gal dancing in that sensational dress is pulsating away a broken heart? Not a chance. Does she have a fantastic time hailing in the New Year? You can bet your best bottle of chilled champagne she does. And so does that new guy in her life. But the morning comes.

The next year when the first Christmas carol floats in the air around me, there will be a moment of euphoria, followed by an abyss of pain, as the memory returns of what I thought we had. The memory floats back of a fantasy when love felt pure and perfect and I thought those spectacular hues of colors would endure forever.

Although other lovers will yet come into my life, when the next Christmas season comes, and the next, and maybe forever, the moment I hear that first Christmas carol, a multi-colored expectation of joy will still explode over me, if only for a millisecond, then fade back into oblivion.

The love songs tell us love is always worth the cost, but the biting-sharp edges on the coral reefs know—it's not always quite that simple.

THIRTY-SIX

PRYING OPEN THE OYSTER SHELL
2006

*L*ike an ocean full of cresting waves, life brims with a multitude of choices.

The choice of selecting pale lavender or muted mauve to accent the bedroom walls.

The choice of taking a chance and going to a dance, or staying home and planting cucumbers.

After so many years of confining restraint, I'm elated to wade into the delectably-widening range of choices.

The choice to go to Santa Monica Beach, where families play in the sand, wearing an emerald-green one-piece swimsuit, or adventure further down the coast to Black's Beach, where nudists frolic in the buff, wearing no swimsuit at all.

The choice of accepting, or not, a man's invitation to fly to Northern California, spend the weekend splashing in a Jacuzzi overlooking the city, ride in a convertible through Sonoma, and taste all the rich wines I can handle.

The choice of whether or not to accept other such escapades.

The choice of whether or not to welcome a new lover into my life.

The choice of how much to reveal about my freeing choices.

Because, after all, that is the nature of choice . . . it's always one's choice.

THIRTY-SEVEN

WAVING FROM THE SHORELINE
2008

*T*here's one thing every mother should be warned about before groaning through the ecstasy of labor pains: Those babies will grow up. There's not much you can do about it, although all the starfish in the sea know I tried.

When my girls were little, I used to push down on their heads and whisper, "Don't grow up, don't grow up," but they didn't listen to me. Little girls are like that. Word on the high seas is little boys are just as bad.

All these years while I've been busy with my life, the day care, and being a mom, my girls have been busy doing just what they should have been doing—growing up. Although my heart wishes they could always stay five years old and need me desperately, those days have vanished forever.

My first splendiferous daughter combines her leadership skills, perseverance, and good grades to earn a scholarship and attend her chosen college out of state. Once she completes her understudies, she transfers to a university, graduates, and falls in love with a handsome young man whom she marries. I'm here to shout the moral to my story for mothers everywhere: Do *not* let your baby girls go to college out of state. Put your foot down and insist they attend a local college. Otherwise, one day, they'll get married and have babies and they'll all live very far away.

My second splendiferous daughter becomes a nurse, travels the world, and falls in love with a handsome young man who lives close to home. They marry. So far, so good. Wait for it. Within a year, they move out of state. The moral of this story is, all a mother can hope for is to buy a car that gets good mileage so she can drive to visit all her grandbabies.

My third splendiferous daughter joins the Navy and survives boot camp (or, more accurately boot camp survives her) near Lake Michigan and then is stationed on the other side of the world. After a short stint stateside, she's deployed to Spain, where—you can already see where this ship is sailing—she meets a handsome Navy man and falls in love. The good news is, after they marry, they return to the States. The bad news is, they don't live anywhere even remotely close to the West Coast. What's a mother to do? Not one damn thing.

Although my daughters were all brought up in the Mormon faith, they have each moved on from the dusty trails of Mormonism and left those convoluted doctrines behind. I'm proud to say each of their world views is much wider and more loving than what they ever heard taught over a Mormon pulpit. Most important of all, they live happy, productive lives.

What more could a mother wish for? Except, of course, that they could all still be five years old again. But that's why God invented grandchildren.

THIRTY-EIGHT

BIG BEAR LAKE ON FATHER'S DAY
2012

*H*appy Father's Day, Dad.

I'm riding my bicycle at Big Bear Lake, thinking of you, trying to figure out how old you'd be if you were still alive. Oh, I wish you were. How fantastic it would be if you showed up around the next corner of the bike path. I wonder what we'd talk about.

Silly question. I know that answer before my feet push the pedals around one more time and before the question finishes forming in my mind. Your favorite topic was always the Book of Mormon. You spent years between its covers. Probably read it hundreds of times. Other men have their Jeeps, football games, or miniature trains, but your passion was always the Book of Mormon.

A brisk breeze smelling of pine sweeps over the lake. I'm bicycling next to my handsome honey who enjoys the mountain air as much as I do. We pedal together up a steep incline. I'm huffing now and let him go ahead as I get lost in thought, but I smile as I remember one of your fondest hopes for the afterlife—an appointment with the last Nephite prophet Moroni, son of Mormon. You had questions, and you wanted answers. You figured, who better to ask than Moroni himself?

You shared a couple of your questions with me. They were good questions—tough questions—but no one seemed to have the answers. You pulled them from the Book of Mormon itself, where some things just didn't quite add up in your analytical mind. I have come to understand those kinds of questions because even tougher Book of Mormon questions have come to light since you have passed on.

Like the questions dealing with the origin of the Book of Abraham, which I never could get past. Tougher still, coming after I left the Church, is the stark evidence provided by DNA against the Book of Mormon claims that the American Indians came from Jerusalem. But those are questions for later generations of Mormons to grapple with—not yours. In some ways, you missed all the excitement.

You taught me to question, and asking my tough questions changed my path. If you would have lived longer, I'm sure you would have joined me on my scriptural journey when I taught Gospel Doctrine. Would your Mormon faith have ended up like mine if we had walked that path together?

One thing I also know, you would understand where I am today, and we'd still love each other just as much.

Perhaps you've heard—word probably gets around up there—it's been ten years since I left the Church. Everything seems to have changed from the way you and I used to talk when I was a child. It was all so simple then.

But now I've learned the value of thinking for myself and claiming my own voice. I've even made a few waves, and that's a good thing. These years have been good ones for me, Dad. I think you'd want to know that. You always wanted what was best for me.

I've inherited your frugal nature for sure, and even if I'm never rich, I've learned to make my sand dollars go farther than any others on the beach. I'm sure you're proud of me. But I've learned that life is about more than watching pennies. It's also about enjoying each day, and I'm doing that, too.

I've made an ocean full of new friends, done more things than I ever thought I would. If you can believe it, I've even jumped out of an airplane. Twice! And I took flying lessons and flew the plane myself. I've hiked many places I never thought I'd see, like Yosemite, Zion, Arches National Parks, and the Wave in Arizona. Being in those beautiful outdoor places always reminds me of when you took our family up in Little Cottonwood Canyon. Now I've hiked more mountain trails than I can count. I figure your knees are so much better now that you have probably hiked miles of trails, too.

I remember one of the things Mom wanted to do before she died— aside from riding an elephant—was to go kayaking. You made sure you granted her wish and took her kayaking in the Provo River. I still have the picture on my vanity. I've gone kayaking, too, and I thought a lot of her while pulling those oars that day, like I'm thinking of you while pushing these pedals today.

I finally retired the day care. It's nice to have a quiet house after all the years of having it filled with the sounds of children. And like you did, I'm even writing a book.

Your granddaughters have grown up beautifully—oh, I wish you and Mom could be here to see them. There's nothing like daughters. They have a better relationship with their dad now, too. We've all grown and learned so much through the years.

And there's more exciting news. I'm finally a grandma of my first little granddaughter, and I'm sure there will be more awesome grandchildren to come. She brings back my own new-mom years and is starting me on a whole new adventure of love. Can you guess what she's going to call me as soon as she's old enough to talk? Merma!

I know if you were standing here next to me, you'd be just as proud of me as you always were, and you would accept the decisions I have made. Maybe that's just another way of saying I'm proud of myself.

I pull hard on my hand brakes and skid to a stop, because right there in front of me, I see it—the spot I've been watching for. The place where the sky and pine trees and lake all come together. Where I feel you and I and nature converge. I grab my smartphone out of my bicycle carrier and take a picture of all of us. I stand here straddling my bike in the middle of the path, breathing in the scene in front of me while I collect my thoughts.

I love you, Dad, and although I'll always continue on my search for answers, I hope you've found the answers to all of yours.

Your loving daughter,

Lorelei

I' pause at Big Bear Lake on Father's Day, 2012.

THIRTY-NINE

UNDERCURRENT OF STRENGTH
2014

*T*he giant structure juts skyward. An azure sky may surround it, clouds may be drifting behind it, but my mind is too focused on the gray facade of the edifice to notice such things. What I *do* notice is the huge rectangular shape of the building, the death-gray pallor of the stone covering it, and the detail of the name chiseled across the front—like a massive headstone.

I've driven over six hundred miles, from Southern California to Salt Lake City, to stand right here and see this for myself.

I drove past the town Nephi, named after a Mormon prophet; past the off-ramp to the town Moroni, named after a Mormon angel; and past the town Lehi, named after a Mormon prophet. I also passed Kolob Canyon Outlook, named after the planet where the Mormon god lives. Try as you might, when you drive through Utah, you just can't escape Mormon theology.

I put my hand in my pocket and run my fingers back and forth, once again, over the folds of the black lace handkerchief. This day has been a long time in coming.

Several hundred people mill around here in City Creek Center, near Temple Square in Salt Lake City. Most of them are dressed like they've just gotten out of church. Except for me. I'm dressed casually in long pants on this hot June day, but I'm sweltering and wish I'd worn shorts.

A small group of women who stand to the right of me burst into laughter at some private joke. A few couples shuffle along the scenic walkway together, and others meander in clusters, visiting.

I stand alone.

The others here have gathered for a vigil to support Kate Kelly, an international human rights lawyer from Washington, D.C. She's sparked a firestorm of controversy by stepping to the front of a group of woman asking the all-male hierarchy of the Mormon Church to consider ordaining women. Her request has been met with threats of excommunication, which will fall upon her head soon enough.

But I'm here for a different reason.

When the others look up at the twenty-eight stories, they see the Church Office Building of the Mormon Church.

I look up and I see a headstone.

When others look up and read, "The Church of Jesus Christ of Latter-day Saints," they see the name of their church.

I look up at the cold font and read the name of the deceased.

Others are here to support Kate.

I'm here to attend a funeral.

A funeral of a close personal friend.

I grew up in Salt Lake City with this friend. A friend I believed in, a friend I devoted my life to, a friend I loved. But after fifty years of service, I discovered this friend had betrayed me. Everywhere I looked, everywhere I studied, I found my friend decomposing into a heap of lies and deceptions, until all that remained were piles of gray, dead, ash. And no one even had the decency to hold a service where I could mourn my loss. Until now. And that's why I'm here.

There's one common thread that binds me to these other women—the handkerchiefs we carry. We will leave them on the front steps of the Church Office Building, and they will be stitched together into a quilt as a remembrance of this event, yet even in this, I stand alone, apart. Because the handkerchief in my pocket is black.

When the handkerchiefs are all carefully sewn into the quilt, how bleakly will my dark one stand out among all the white, pastel and flowered ones? Will anyone look at my stark square of black and think of death?

It doesn't matter if anyone understands. It matters only to me. So with unfaltering steps, I move to the threshold of the epic structure. I stand erect and toss my black flower down on the grave of my childhood faith.

And step away.

FORTY

A NEW LORELEI

*P*erhaps my epitaph will say, *She should have spent more time at the beach.*

It's true I've spent much more of my life in a Mormon church than on a beach, but that's all behind me now. For over five decades, I've lived the Mormon lifestyle: attended enough meetings to last fourteen light years, baked enough casseroles to feed a pod of whales, and paid enough tithing to commandeer a pirate ship. All under the direction of the almighty Mormon male. I didn't know any other way. Until, week by week, I studied my way out.

Now, as I stroll along this magnificent beach under a sun sliding down through coral clouds, I know there's a better way to live.

The sound of slapping water echoes in my ears as a chilly sea breeze whips around me. The surf pounds her white-edged fists into the sandy beach. Seagulls shriek and circle above me, flapping through their frantic air dance as particles of sand attach themselves to the soles of my feet.

A wave washes up and splatters on my cheek. As I touch the wetness, memories engulf me of my dad and our discussions of family, logic, religion, poetry, life—and his tale of the Lorelei.

The water whispers of transformation.

While a Mormon, I trekked blindly behind my patriarchal leaders.

As a Mermaid, I'll torpedo through ocean currents, shaping my own trails, trusting an inner compass to chart my course.

While a Mormon, I lived fearful of the power of passion.

As a Mermaid, I'll fiercely claim my passion for logic, literature, moonlight, and lovers.

While a Mormon, I lived bound in ropes of twisted laws.

As a Mermaid, I'll flap my tail with bravado and explore the mysteries of the sea.

My moment of metamorphosis is here. The water calls. A wave builds momentum, changes into a curling wall of wetness and roars toward me. I plunge into its white froth. As the waters of the eternal sea pulse all around, I propel my new self forward, break though the giant wave, and ferociously claim my new life.

Free!

THANK YOU FOR READING!

Dear Reader,

I hope you enjoyed *From Mormon to Mermaid*.

As an author, I love feedback. So tell me what you thought about this book. I'd love to hear from you. You can write me at

frommormontomermaid@gmail.com
and visit me on the web at
www.frommormontomermaid.com.

Finally, I need to ask a favor. If you're so inclined, I'd love a review of *From Mormon to Mermaid*. What did you like most? The least? What about the book surprised you? Whatever your comments, I'd just enjoy your feedback. Reviews can be tough to come by these days, and you, the reader, have the power to make or break a book. You can leave your review at Amazon.com.

Thank you so much for reading *From Mormon to Mermaid* and for spending time with me.

Lorelei

APPENDIX A

<u>Chapter One, THE LORELEI</u>
How the Book of Mormon came to be—think boats carrying Jews from across the sea

Introduction to the Book of Mormon: "The record gives an account of two great civilizations. One came from Jerusalem in 600 B.C., and afterward separated into two nations, known as the Nephites and the Lamanites. The other came much earlier when the Lord confounded the tongues at the Tower of Babel. This group is known as the Jaredites. After thousands of years, all were destroyed except the Lamanites, and they are the principal ancestors of the American Indians."

How God came to be—or, thank God if you're a man, for you can be a god

> As man is, God once was; as God is, man may be. (LDS Apostle James E. Talmage, Articles of Faith, pp. 430-431, LDS Collectors Library '97 CD-ROM)

> Here, then, is eternal life — to know the only wise and true God; and you have got to learn how to be Gods yourselves, and to be kings and priests to God, the same as all Gods have done before you ... To inherit the same power, the same glory and the same exaltation, until you arrive at the station of a God. (LDS President Joseph Smith, *History of the Church,* Vol. 6, p. 306, LDS Collectors Library '97 CD-ROM)

Then shall they be gods, because they have no end; therefore shall they be from everlasting to everlasting, because they continue; then shall they be above all, because all things are subject unto them. Then shall they be gods, because they have all power, and the angels are subject unto them. (*Doctrine & Covenants* 132:20)

Mystery solved—the planet where God lives

God lives on or near the planet Kolob with his many wives. Abraham "saw the stars, that they were very great, and that one of them was nearest unto the throne of God; and the name of the great one is Kolob, because it is near unto me, for I am the Lord thy God: I have set this one to govern all those which belong to the same order as that upon which thou standest." (Book of Abraham 3:2-3) See chapter Twenty-two of *From Mormon to Mermaid*.

In Mormon Sunday school, we would sing about Kolob, the planet where God lives, in hymn number 284.

Chapter Two, HOOK, LINE, AND THINKER
Remember, when the prophet speaks, the thinking is done
Heber C. Kimball, one of the original twelve apostles with Joseph Smith and first counselor to Brigham Young, said,

"WAKE UP, YE ELDERS OF ISRAEL, and live to God and none else; and learn to do as you are told, both old and young: learn to do as you are told for the future . . . if you are told by your leader to do a thing, do it. None of your business whether it is right or wrong." (*Journal of Discourses*, November 8, 1857, Vol. 6, p. 32)

This is brought home quite clearly in Elder Dallin H. Oaks' statement in a PBS interview: "I also said something else that has excited people: that it's wrong to criticize leaders of the Church, even if the criticism is true, because it diminishes their effectiveness as a servant of the Lord." (http://www.pbs.org/mormons/etc/script2.html)

Some of the prophetic quotes I struggled with

Suppose you found your brother in bed with your wife, and put a javelin through both of them, you would be justified, and they would atone for their sins, and be received into the kingdom of God. I would at once do so in such a case; and under such circumstances, I have no wife whom I love so well that I would not put a javelin through her heart, and I would do it with clean hands. (Second Prophet Brigham Young, Blood Atonement Sermon, *Journal of Discourses*, Vol. 3, 1856, p. 247)

There are sins that men commit for which they cannot receive forgiveness in this world, or in that which is to come, and if they had their eyes open to see their true condition, they would be perfectly willing to have their blood spilt upon the ground that the smoke thereof might ascend to heaven as an offering for their sins; and the smoking incense would atone for their sins, whereas, if such is not the case, they will stick to them and remain upon them in the spirit world. (Sermon by Brigham Young, *Journal of Discourses*, Vol. 4, 1856, pages 53-54, also published in the *Deseret News* newspaper, 1856)

... the one-wife system not only degenerates the human family, both physically and intellectually, but it is entirely incompatible with philosophical notions and has always proved a curse to a people. (Third Prophet John Taylor, *Millennial Star*, Vol. 15, 1853, p. 227)

Chapter Three, *DAM* THE EQUALITY

Numerous divorces can be traced directly to the day when the wife left the home and went out into the world into employment. Two incomes raise the standard of living beyond its norm. Two spouses working prevent the complete and proper home life, break into the family prayers, create an independence which is not cooperative, causes distortion, limits the family, and frustrates the children already born. (Spencer W. Kimball, San Antonio Fireside, December 3, 1977)

No bishop, no missionary should ever hesitate or lack the faith to teach the law of tithing to the poor. The sentiment of 'They can't *afford* to' needs to be replaced with 'They can't afford *not* to.' One of the first things a bishop *must* do to help the needy is ask them to pay their tithing. Like the widow, if a destitute family is faced with the decision of paying their tithing or eating, they should pay their tithing. The bishop can help them with their food and other basic needs until they become self-reliant. ("Tithing—a Commandment Even for the Destitute," Lynn G. Robbins of the Seventy, *Ensign*, May 2005, p. 34)

Is it a Church or a corporation?

The Church has organized several tax-exempt corporations to handle the transfer of money and capital. These include the Corporation of the Presiding Bishop of the Church of Jesus Christ of Latter-day Saints, which was organized in 1916 according to the laws of Utah to acquire, hold, and dispose of real property. In 1923, the Church incorporated the Corporation of the President of the Church of Jesus Christ of Latter-day Saints in Utah in order to receive and manage money and Church donations. In 1997, the Church incorporated Intellectual Reserve, Inc., to hold all of the Church's copyrights, trademark, and other intellectual property. The Church also has several other non-tax-exempt corporations, such as Bonneville International, and the *Deseret News.*

Below is the beginning of a thorough discussion from the blog "By Common Dissent" by Matthew Bryde posted on March 9, 2015, titled "The Corporation we call a 'Church.'"

When reading posts on Facebook and Reddit and other discussion boards, you often come across terms such as "*Morg*" and "*TSCC*" (*"The So Called Church"*). Why do people refer to the Mormon church with these terms and what do they mean? Well after some digging around I soon discovered that "The Church of Jesus Christ of Latter-day Saints", is no longer a "*church*" and has not been since 1890, when the US government disincorporated it.

The actual "church" that Joseph Smith established back in 1830 no longer exists as such. What we think of as "The Church of Jesus Christ of Latter-day Saints" (hereafter referred to as "*The Church*™"), exists today as a trademark, owned by a subsidiary of a corporation known as "*The Corporation of the President of The Church of Jesus Christ of Latter-day Saints*".

So technically, there are no members of "*The Church*™", despite the common usage whereby people call themselves members. The actual church that used to go by that name, and which claims Jesus Christ as its head, does not exist today in any legally recognized form.

But, I'm getting ahead of myself. Let's look at the history…

To read the rest of the blog, go to:
http://bycommondissent.org/2015/03/09/the-corporation-we-call-a-church/

Take a guess—how much money does the Mormon Church have?

"The estimated grand total of LDS assets, by a conservative reckoning, would be $25—30 billion." Richard N. Ostling and Joan K. Ostling *Mormon America, The Power and the Promise*, 2007, p. 118.

> If you were to construct a religion as a business, it would be hard to beat the LDS Church. From its mandatory tithing for access to sacred Temples to its spiritual blessing on business and wealth accumulation and its tax-friendly admixture of for-profit and not-for-profit enterprises, it is the Prosperity Gospel with better accountants. And that makes it the quintessential religion for America - giving the New World a place in the Gospels, bringing the Garden of Eden to Missouri, and providing a divine blessing for American free enterprise. All it needs is a president of the United States to broaden its appeal in a fusion of faith and country. It's been trying since Joseph

Smith ran for the highest office in the land - not a typical path for a "spiritual" leader. Now, as the unofficial religion of American capitalism in its least regulated and most rapacious form, it has its chance. (Andrew Sullivan, The Daily Beast
 http://andrewsullivan.thedailybeast.com/2012/07/capitalism-as-a-religion.html)

Bloomberg Business Week Features
How the Mormons Make Money
By Caroline Winter
July 10, 2012

Mormons make up only 1.4 percent of the U.S. population, but the church's holdings are vast. First among its for-profit enterprises is DMC, which reaps estimated annual revenues of $1.2 billion from six subsidiaries, according to the business information and analysis firm Hoover's Company Records (DNB).

Those subsidiaries run a newspaper, 11 radio stations, a TV station, a publishing and distribution company, a digital media company, a hospitality business, and an insurance business with assets worth $3.3 billion.

AgReserves, another for-profit Mormon umbrella company, together with other church-run agricultural affiliates, reportedly owns roughly 1 million acres in the continental U.S., on which the church has farms, hunting preserves, orchards, and ranches. These include the $1 billion 290,000-acre Deseret Ranches in Florida, which, in addition to keeping 44,000 cows and 1,300 bulls, also has citrus, sod, and timber operations. Outside the U.S., AgReserves operates in Britain, Canada, Australia, Mexico, Argentina, and Brazil. Its Australian property, valued at $61 million in 1997, has estimated annual sales of $276 million, according to Dun & Bradstreet.

The church also runs several for-profit real estate arms that own, develop, and manage malls, parking lots, office parks, residential buildings, and more. Hawaii Reserve, for example, owns or manages more than 7,000 acres on Oahu, where it maintains commercial and residential buildings, parks, water and sewage infrastructure, and a cemetery. Utah Property Management Associates, a real estate arm of the church, manages portions of the City Creek Mall. According to Spencer P. Eccles from the Utah Governor's Office of Economic Development, the mall cost the church an estimated $2 billion. It is only one part of a $5 billion church-funded revamping of downtown Salt Lake City, according to the Mormon-owned news site KSL. 'They run their businesses like businesses, no bones about it,' says Eccles.

The church also owns several nonprofit organizations, some of which appear to be lucrative. Take, for example, the Polynesian Cultural Center (PCC), a 42-acre tropical theme park on Oahu's north shore that hosts luaus, canoe rides, and tours through seven simulated Polynesian villages. General-admission adult tickets cost $49.95; VIP tickets cost up to $228.95. In 2010 the PCC had net assets worth $70 million and collected $23 million in ticket sales alone, as well as $36 million in tax-free donations. The PCC's president, meanwhile, received a salary of $296,000. At the local level, the PCC, opened in 1963, began paying commercial property taxes in 1992, when the Land and Tax Appeal Court of Hawaii ruled that the theme park 'is not for charitable purposes' and is, in fact, a 'commercial enterprise, and business undertaking.'

Nevertheless, the tourist destination remains exempt from federal taxes, because the PCC claims to be a 'living museum' and an education-oriented charity that employs students who work at the center to pay their way through church-run Brigham Young University-Hawaii.

According to U.S. law, religions have no obligation to open their books to the public, and the LDS Church officially stopped reporting any finances in the early 1960s. In 1997 an investigation by *Time* used cross-religious comparisons and internal information to estimate the church's total value at $30 billion. The magazine also produced an estimate that $5 billion worth of tithing flows into the church annually, and that it owned at least $6 billion in stocks and bonds. The Mormon Church at the time said the estimates were grossly exaggerated, but a recent investigation by Reuters in collaboration with sociology professor Cragun estimates that the LDS Church is likely worth $40 billion today and collects up to $8 billion in tithing each year.

Quinn, a faithful Mormon who spent 12 years on the faculty at the LDS Church's Brigham Young University in Provo, Utah, before being excommunicated for apostasy related to research he published on Mormons, has been gathering financial information for years. Several high-ranking church insiders told him that the church's finances are so compartmentalized that no single person, not even the president, knows the entirety of its holdings.

The Associated Press, on Monday, July 28, 1997, reported,

> The Mormon Church is the most prosperous of American religions and is preparing to focus that considerable wealth on an unprecedented campaign of international expansion, according to a cover story in *Time* magazine on newsstands this week." According to the same article, the estimated total income from tithes and other offerings is $5.9 billion a year. Estimated total income from business investments is $600 million a year. The church's total assets was placed at a minimum of $30 billion and as a corporation, its estimated 5.9 billion in annual gross income would place it midway through the Fortune 500. "There is no major church in the U.S. as active as the Latter-day Saints in economic life, nor, per capita, as successful at it," the story said.

Chapter Five, ANCHOR OF FAITH

Los Angeles Times
Mormon Church Apologizes for Posthumous Baptisms
By Mitchell Landsberg
February 15, 2012

The parents of Nazi hunter Simon Wiesenthal received the rite, which was also sought for relatives of Holocaust survivor Elie Wiesel. Critics note that Mormons agreed in 1995 to stop baptizing Jewish victims of the Holocaust.

The Mormon Church apologized Tuesday for a "serious breach of protocol" after it was discovered that the parents of the late Nazi hunter Simon Wiesenthal were posthumously baptized as Mormons. The church also acknowledged that one of its members tried to baptize posthumously three relatives of Holocaust survivor Elie Wiesel.

The efforts, at least in Wiesenthal's case, violated the terms of an agreement that the church signed in 1995, in which it agreed to stop baptizing Jewish victims of the Holocaust. Wiesenthal and Wiesel gained fame for careers spent grappling with the legacy of the Holocaust, Wiesenthal by hunting down war criminals, Wiesel by writing books that became part of the canon of 20th century literature.

And the problem with Mormons marrying the dead—there's always the possibility they'd rather still be divorced.

How Mary and God the Father created Jesus—the old-fashioned way

> When the time came that His first-born, the Saviour, should come into the world and take a tabernacle, the Father came Himself and favoured that spirit [Mary] with a tabernacle instead of letting any other man do it. The Savior was begotten by the Father of His spirit, by the same Being who is the Father of our spirits, and that is all the organic difference between Jesus Christ and you and me. (Prophet Brigham Young, *Journal of Discourses*, Vol. 4, p. 218)

> Therefore, the Father and Mother of Jesus, according to the flesh, must have been associated together in the capacity of Husband and Wife; hence the Virgin Mary must have been, for the time being, the lawful wife of God the Father;... Inasmuch as God was the first husband to her, it may be that He only gave her to be the wife of Joseph while in this mortal state, and that He intended after the resurrection to again take her as one of his own wives to raise up immortal spirits in eternity. (Apostle Orson Pratt, *The Seer*, 1853, p. 158)

Really—God is a polygamist?

> ... the great Messiah who was the founder of the Christian religion, was a polygamist,... the Messiah chose to take upon himself his seed; and by marrying many honorable wives himself, show to all future generations that he approbated the plurality of Wives ... God the Father had a plurality of wives ... the Son followed the example of his Father, and became the great Bridegroom to whom kings' daughters and many honorable Wives were to be married. We have also proved that both God the Father and our Lord Jesus Christ inherit their wives in eternity as well as in time;... (Apostle Orson Pratt, *The Seer*, 1853, p. 172)

"If none but Gods will be permitted to multiply immortal children, it follows that each God must have one or more wives." said LDS Apostle Orson Pratt, in *The Seer*, 1853, p. 158.

Chapter Eight, THE UNDERTOW OF UNDERWEAR
Why Mormons wear—that underwear

Church members who have been clothed with the garment in the temple have made a covenant to wear it throughout their lives. This means it is worn as underclothing both day and night:

> The promise of protection and blessings is conditioned upon worthiness and faithfulness in keeping the covenant. Members of the Church wear the garment as a reminder of the sacred covenants they have made with the Lord and also as a protection against temptation and evil. How it is worn is an outward expression of an inward commitment to follow the Savior. (Letter of the First Presidency, 10 October 1988)

> Each individual should be provided with the endowment clothing they need. The garments must be clean and white, and of the approved pattern; they must not be altered or mutilated, and are to be

worn as intended, down to the wrist and ankles, and around the neck. These requirements are imperative; admission to the Temple will be refused to those who do not comply therewith. - *President Joseph F. Smith, "Instructions Concerning Temple Ordinance Work," President of the Salt Lake Temple 1898-1911*

Because women were not originally intended to be a part of the endowment ceremony, when they were finally admitted, women received the same garment as did men. Women and men in the Church wore the same garments in the temple until 1965, so all Mormon pioneer women wore the men's garment, which were 100% cotton long johns.

As early as the 1890s, LDS women tried getting their own garment pattern, but to no avail.

See http://www.i4m.com/think/temples/mormon-garments.htm

Don't sleep in the buff. Be able to answer yes to Temple Recommend when the bishop asks, "If you have previously received your temple endowment: Do you keep the covenants that you made in the temple? Do you wear the garment both night and day as instructed in the endowment and in accordance with the covenant you made in the temple?"

Want more information on the temple ceremony—or a comparison with Masonry?

See *Mormon America, The Power and the Promise, Rituals Sacred and Secret,* by Richard N. Ostling and Joan K. Ostling (2007, pp. 188-206)

Also: http://en.wikipedia.org/wiki/Mormonism_and_Freemasonry

http://www.ldsendowment.org/masonry.html
http://mormoncurtain.com/topic_masons.html

Joseph Smith admitted to being a Mason

Joseph's journal entry for March 15, 1842, states, "In the evening I received the first degree in Free Masonry in the Nauvoo Lodge, assembled in my general business office." (*History of the Church* Vol. 4, p. 551). The next day, his journal entry noted he became a Master Mason, "I was with the Masonic Lodge and rose to the sublime degree." (*History of the Church* Vol. 4, p. 552).

Dr. Reed Durham, who was president of the Mormon History Association, noted:

> There is absolutely no question in my mind that the Mormon ceremony which came to be known as the Endowment, introduced by Joseph Smith to Mormon Masons, had an immediate inspiration from Masonry. It is also obvious that the Nauvoo Temple architecture was in part, at least, Masonically influenced. Indeed, it appears that there was an intentional attempt to utilize Masonic symbols and motifs. (Presidential address at the Mormon History Association Convention, April 20, 1974, *Mormon Miscellaneous*, pub. David C. Martin, October, 1975, pp. 11-16)

Less than two months after becoming a Master Mason, Joseph introduced the endowment ceremony. When the Masonic rites of Freemasonry and the endowment temple ceremony are compared, they're very similar. In fact, parts are identical.

Chapter Nine, KICKING UP YOUR TAIL
Why we didn't know the in-and-out rules—of marital sex

The following letter from the Mormon Prophet Harold B. Lee to an anonymous member, was not made available to the general Church membership, but shows the beliefs that would later be given to bishops to counsel married couples and to determine if they were worthy of going to the temple —*but*—couples weren't told in advance about it.

I was shocked to have you raise the question about "'oral lovemaking in the genital area among married couples." Heaven forbid any such degrading activities which would be abhorrent in the sight of the Lord. For any Latter-day Saint, and particularly those who have been taught in the sacred ordinances of the temple, to engage in any kind of perversions of this sacred God-given gift of procreation, would be sure to bring down the condemnation of the Lord whom we would offend were we to engage in any such practice. (May 17, 1973, prepared by President Lee's secretary)

The next letter was then sent to all male leaders—not the general Church—so the rest of us still didn't know we were supposed to "keep our mouths shut."

Married persons should understand that if in their marital relations they are guilty of unnatural, impure, or unholy practices, they should not enter the temple unless and until they repent and discontinue any such practices. Husbands and wives who are aware of these requirements can determine by themselves their standing before the Lord. All of this should be conveyed without having priesthood leaders focus upon intimate matters which are a part of husband and wife relationships. Skillful interviewing and counseling can occur without discussion of clinical details by placing firm responsibility on individual members of the Church to put their lives in order before exercising the privilege of entering a house of the Lord. *The First Presidency has interpreted oral sex as constituting an unnatural, impure, or unholy practice.* If a person is engaged in a practice which troubles him enough to ask about it, he should discontinue it. (Letter to all Priesthood Leaders, January 5, 1982, signed by Prophet Spencer Kimball, N. Eldon Tanner, Marion D. Romney, and Gordon B. Hinkley, who would become the thirteenth prophet. Emphasis added)

Chapter Eleven, FISH STORY — the One That *Should* Have Gotten Away

Could it be—racism I see?

You see some classes of the human family that are black, uncouth, uncomely, disagreeable and low in their habits, wild, and seemingly deprived of nearly all the blessings of the intelligence that is generally bestowed upon mankind . . . Cain slew his brother. Cain might have been killed, and that would have put a termination to that line of human beings. This was not to be, and the Lord put a mark upon him, which is the flat nose and black skin. (Second Mormon Prophet Brigham Young, *Journal of Discourses*, Vol. 7, p. 290).

Shall I tell you the law of God in regard to the African race? If the white man who belongs to the chosen seed mixes his blood with the seed of Cain, the penalty, under the law of God, is death on the spot. This will always be so. (Second Mormon Prophet Brigham Young, Journal *of Discourses*, Volume 10, p. 110.)

Below is the statement the Church issued five days after the death of Nelson Mandela intended to distance the Church from racism. It's buried in so much ink, you would miss an apology if you were to look for it. But not to worry, even if you take the time to dig through it, you won't find a hint of an apology anywhere, or a recanting of past statements by Mormon prophets.

Here it is in its full corporation-style glory in case you're inclined to wade through it (See footnotes referenced at: //www.lds.org/topics/race-and-the-priesthood?lang=eng):

December 10, 2013
Race and the Priesthood

In theology and practice, The Church of Jesus Christ of Latter-day Saints embraces the universal human family. Latter-day Saint scripture and teachings affirm that God loves all of His children and makes salvation available to all. God created the many diverse races and ethnicities and esteems them all equally. As the Book of Mormon puts it, "all are alike unto God."[1]

The structure and organization of the Church encourage racial integration. Latter-day Saints attend Church services according to the geographical boundaries of their local ward, or congregation. By definition, this means that the racial, economic, and demographic composition of Mormon congregations generally mirrors that of the wider local community.[2] The Church's lay ministry also tends to facilitate integration: a black bishop may preside over a mostly white congregation; a Hispanic woman may be paired with an Asian woman to visit the homes of a racially diverse membership. Church members of different races and ethnicities regularly minister in one another's homes and serve alongside one another as teachers, as youth leaders, and in myriad other assignments in their local congregations. Such practices make The Church of Jesus Christ of Latter-day Saints a thoroughly integrated faith.

Despite this modern reality, for much of its history—from the mid-1800s until 1978—the Church did not ordain men of black African descent to its priesthood or allow black men or women to participate in temple endowment or sealing ordinances.

The Church was established in 1830, during an era of great racial division in the United States. At the time, many people of African descent lived in slavery, and racial distinctions and prejudice were not just common but customary among white Americans. Those realities, though unfamiliar and disturbing today, influenced all aspects of people's lives, including their religion. Many Christian churches of that era, for instance, were segregated along racial lines. From the beginnings of the Church, people of every race and ethnicity could be baptized and received as members. Toward the end of his life, Church founder Joseph Smith openly opposed slavery. There has never been a Churchwide policy of segregated congregations.[3]

During the first two decades of the Church's existence, a few black men were ordained to the priesthood. One of these men, Elijah Abel, also participated in temple ceremonies in Kirtland, Ohio, and was later baptized as proxy for deceased relatives in Nauvoo, Illinois. There is no evidence that any black men were denied the priesthood during Joseph Smith's lifetime.

In 1852, President Brigham Young publicly announced that men of black African descent could no longer be ordained to the priesthood, though thereafter blacks continued to join the Church through baptism and receiving the gift of the Holy Ghost. Following the death of Brigham Young, subsequent Church presidents restricted blacks from receiving the temple endowment or being married in the temple. Over time, Church leaders and members advanced many theories to explain the priesthood and temple restrictions. None of these explanations is accepted today as the official doctrine of the Church.

The Church in an American Racial Culture

The Church of Jesus Christ of Latter-day Saints was restored amidst a highly contentious racial culture in which whites were afforded great privilege. In 1790, the U.S. Congress limited citizenship to "free white person[s]."[4] Over the next half century, issues of race divided the country — while slave labor was legal in the more agrarian South, it was eventually banned in the more urbanized North. Even so, racial discrimination was widespread in the North as well as the South, and many states implemented laws banning interracial marriage.[5] In 1857, the U.S. Supreme Court declared that blacks possessed "no rights which the white man was bound to respect."[6] A generation after the Civil War (1861–65) led to the end of slavery in the United States, the U.S. Supreme Court ruled that "separate but equal" facilities for blacks and whites were constitutional, a decision that legalized a host of public color barriers until the Court reversed itself in 1954.[7]

In 1850, the U.S. Congress created Utah Territory, and the U.S. president appointed Brigham Young to the position of territorial governor. Southerners who had converted to the Church and migrated to Utah with their slaves raised the question of slavery's legal status in the territory. In two speeches delivered before the Utah territorial legislature in January and February 1852, Brigham Young announced a policy restricting men of black African descent from priesthood ordination. At the same time, President Young said that at some future day, black Church members would "have [all] the privilege and more" enjoyed by other members.[8]

The justifications for this restriction echoed the widespread ideas about racial inferiority that had been used to argue for the legalization of black "servitude" in the Territory of Utah.[9] According to one view, which had been promulgated in the United States from at least the 1730s, blacks descended from the same lineage as the biblical Cain, who slew his brother Abel.[10] Those who accepted this view believed that God's "curse" on Cain was the mark of a dark skin. Black servitude was sometimes viewed as a second curse placed upon Noah's grandson Canaan as a result of Ham's indiscretion toward his father.[11] Although slavery was not a significant factor in Utah's economy and was soon abolished, the restriction on priesthood ordinations remained.

Removing the Restriction

Even after 1852, at least two black Mormons continued to hold the priesthood. When one of these men, Elijah Abel, petitioned to receive his temple endowment in 1879, his request was denied. Jane Manning James, a faithful black member who crossed the plains and lived in Salt Lake City until her death in 1908, similarly asked to enter the temple; she was allowed to perform baptisms for the dead for her ancestors but was not allowed to participate in other ordinances.[12] The curse of Cain was often put forward as justification for the priesthood and temple restrictions. Around the turn of the century, another explanation gained currency: blacks were said to have been less than fully valiant in the premortal battle against Lucifer and, as a consequence, were restricted from priesthood and temple blessings.[13]

By the late 1940s and 1950s, racial integration was becoming more common in American life. Church President David O. McKay emphasized that the restriction extended only to men of black African descent. The Church had always allowed Pacific Islanders to hold the priesthood, and President McKay clarified that black Fijians and Australian Aborigines could also be ordained to the priesthood and instituted missionary work among them. In South Africa, President McKay reversed a prior policy that required prospective priesthood holders to trace their lineage out of Africa.[14]

Nevertheless, given the long history of withholding the priesthood from men of black African descent, Church leaders believed that a revelation from God was needed to alter the policy, and they made ongoing efforts to understand what should be done. After praying for guidance, President McKay did not feel impressed to lift the ban.[15]

As the Church grew worldwide, its overarching mission to "go ye therefore, and teach all nations"[16] seemed increasingly incompatible with the priesthood and temple restrictions. The Book of Mormon declared that the gospel message of salvation should go forth to "every nation, kindred, tongue, and people."[17] While there were no limits on whom the Lord invited to "partake of his goodness" through baptism,[18] the priesthood and temple restrictions created significant barriers, a point made increasingly evident as the Church spread in international locations with diverse and mixed racial heritages.

Brazil in particular presented many challenges. Unlike the United States and South Africa where legal and de facto racism led to deeply segregated societies, Brazil prided itself on its open, integrated, and mixed racial heritage. In 1975, the Church announced that a temple would be built in São Paulo, Brazil. As the temple construction proceeded, Church authorities encountered faithful black and mixed-ancestry Mormons who had contributed financially and in other ways to the building of the São Paulo temple, a sanctuary they realized they would not be allowed to enter once it was completed. Their sacrifices, as well as the conversions of thousands of Nigerians and Ghanaians in the 1960s and early 1970s, moved Church leaders.[19]

Church leaders pondered promises made by prophets such as Brigham Young that black members would one day receive priesthood and temple blessings. In June 1978, after "spending many hours in the Upper Room of the [Salt Lake] Temple supplicating the Lord for divine guidance," Church President Spencer W. Kimball, his counselors in the First Presidency, and members of the Quorum of the Twelve Apostles received a revelation. "He has heard our prayers, and by revelation has confirmed that the long-promised day has come," the First Presidency announced on June 8. The First Presidency stated that they were "aware of the promises made by the prophets and presidents of the Church who have preceded us" that "all of our brethren who are worthy may receive the priesthood."[20] The revelation rescinded the restriction on priesthood ordination. It also extended the blessings of the temple to all worthy Latter-day Saints, men and women. The First Presidency statement regarding the revelation was canonized in the Doctrine and Covenants as Official Declaration 2.

This "revelation on the priesthood," as it is commonly known in the Church, was a landmark revelation and a historic event. Those who were present at the time described it in reverent terms. Gordon B. Hinckley, then a member of the Quorum of the Twelve, remembered it this way: "There was a hallowed and sanctified atmosphere in the room. For me, it felt as if a conduit opened between the heavenly throne and the kneeling, pleading prophet of God who was joined by his Brethren. ... Every man in that circle, by the power of the Holy Ghost, knew the same thing. ... Not one of us who was present on that occasion was ever quite the same after that. Nor has the Church been quite the same."[21]

Reaction worldwide was overwhelmingly positive among Church members of all races. Many Latter-day Saints wept for joy at the news. Some reported feeling a collective weight lifted from their shoulders. The Church began priesthood ordinations for men of African descent immediately, and black men and women entered temples throughout the world. Soon after the revelation, Elder Bruce R. McConkie, an apostle, spoke of new "light and knowledge" that had erased previously "limited understanding."[22]

The Church Today

Today, the Church disavows the theories advanced in the past that black skin is a sign of divine disfavor or curse, or that it reflects actions in a premortal life; that mixed-race marriages are a sin; or that blacks or people of any other race or ethnicity are inferior in any way to anyone else. Church leaders today unequivocally condemn all racism, past and present, in any form.[23]

Since that day in 1978, the Church has looked to the future, as membership among Africans, African Americans and others of African descent has continued to grow rapidly. While Church records for individual members do not indicate an individual's race or ethnicity, the number of Church members of African descent is now in the hundreds of thousands.

The Church proclaims that redemption through Jesus Christ is available to the entire human family on the conditions God has prescribed. It affirms that God is "no respecter of persons"[24] and emphatically declares that anyone who is righteous—regardless of race—is favored of Him. The teachings of the Church in relation to God's children are epitomized by a verse in the second book of Nephi: "[The Lord] denieth none that cometh unto him, black and white, bond and free, male and female; ... all are alike unto God, both Jew and Gentile."[25]

Chapter Twelve, CHILLING
Be a polygamist—or be damned.

"Now if any of you will deny the plurality of wives, and continue to do so, I promise that you will be damned." (Second Prophet Brigham Young, *Journal of Discourses*, Vol. 3, p. 266).

Brigham Young declared, "The only men who become Gods, even the Sons of God, are those who enter into polygamy." (*Journal of Discourses*, August 19, 1866, Vol. 11, p. 269)

> In the early days of this dispensation, as part of the promised restitution of all things, the Lord revealed the principle of plural marriage to the Prophet ... Obviously the holy practice will commence again after the Second Coming of the Son of Man and the ushering in of the millennium. (Apostle Bruce R. McConkie, *Mormon Doctrine, p.* 578)

Men may have millions of wives and children—why settle for less?

> "Brother Cannon remarked that people wondered how many wives and children I had. He may inform them, that I shall have wives and children by the million, and glory, and riches and power and dominion, and kingdom after kingdom, and reign triumphantly." (Second Prophet Brigham Young, *Journal of Discourses*, Vol. 8, p. 178).

> Supposing that I have a wife or a dozen of them, and she should say, "You cannot be exalted without me" and suppose they all should say "so, what of that?" Suppose that I lose the whole of them before I go into the spirit world, but that I have been a good, faithful man ... do you think I will be destitute there. No, the Lord says there are more there than there are here ... there are millions of them ... we will go to

brother Joseph [Smith], and say, "Here we are brother Joseph; we are here ourselves are we not, with none of the property we possessed in our probationary state, not even the rings on our fingers"' He will say to us, "Come along, my boys, we will give you a good suit of clothes. Where are your wives?" "They are back yonder; they would not follow us." "Never mind" says Joseph. "Here are thousands, have all you want." (LDS First Presidency Heber C. Kimball, *Journal of Discourses*, Vol. 4, p. 209)

Remember what I said about Mormons really not knowing about the essays on lds.org that explained the ban on blacks being a misunderstanding? It gets better. This Mormon Sunday school teacher was dismissed for using that church's race essay in his lesson:

The Salt Lake Tribune
Religion: Sunday School Instructor Dismissed After He Tapped Faith's Writings to Talk About Race and Priesthood
Peggy Fletcher Stack
The Salt Lake Tribune
May 5, 2015

It all started with a question.

The Mormon youth simply asked his white Sunday school teacher why the man's Nigerian wife and her family would join a church that had barred blacks from being ordained to its all-male priesthood until 1978. Why, the student wanted to know, was the ban instituted in the first place?

To answer the teen's inquiry, Brian Dawson turned to the Utah-based faith's own materials, including its groundbreaking 2013 essay, "Race and the Priesthood." His research prompted an engaging discussion with his class of 12- to 14-year-olds.

But it didn't please his local lay leaders, who removed him from his teaching assignment — even though the essay has been approved by top Mormon leaders and appears on the church's official website lds.org.

The Church of Jesus Christ of Latter-day Saints declined to comment on the handling of the Sunday school incident, but reiterated its efforts to spread the word about the race article and its other essays on Mormon history and theology.

The LDS Church "has communicated the value of these essays in many ways, including direct correspondence to priesthood leaders," spokesman Doug Andersen says. "In addition, church-owned media, social-media sharing and Facebook have been effective in making these essays more widely available. The essays are also translated into numerous languages."

Nonetheless, the essay on race, says Tamu Smith, co-author of "Diary of Two Mad Black Mormons," is not all that familiar to the LDS faithful and, often, their congregational leaders.

"The majority of the church doesn't know about it," says Smith, who has traveled the country for book signings and speaking events. "My former stake president in Provo would not have known about it, either, if I hadn't called it to his attention."

Despite the essay being included in the latest curriculum for LDS high school and college students, she says, "many seminary teachers [for high school], institute [college] teachers, and even some people teaching at Brigham Young University are blind to it — even when you point things out to them."

It's "great" that the essay is on the church website, Smith says, "but people don't believe it."

It was neither signed nor penned by the governing First Presidency, nor has it been mentioned, alluded to, or footnoted in speeches by LDS authorities at the faith's semiannual General Conferences.

Smith is all in favor of speaking openly about black Mormon history, especially at church meetings, and acknowledging mistakes — even by LDS leaders.

"You would think bishops and stake presidents would have a vested interest in telling the truth about history," she says. "Sometimes, they act like they don't — because they're afraid."

Dawson, however, has no such fear.

Psychologist warns of psychological problems of teaching Church youth that Joseph Smith's marrying teenagers was justified:

The Salt Lake Tribune
Think, Seminary Teachers, Before Acceding to Church Essay on Joseph Smith's Polygamy
Kristy Money
March 28 2015

Months ago I wrote an op-ed addressed to the writers of the LDS Gospel Topics essay on Joseph Smith's polygamy, asking them to consider rephrasing that Joseph's marriage to a 14-year-old — among other troubling aspects — was a mistake. I mentioned my concerns as a psychologist, which originated from hearing the essay would soon be incorporated into youth and LDS seminary curriculum.

And so it has. This upcoming week, 14- to 18-year-old youth will learn in seminary a revised lesson on D&C Section 132 (the section outlining the modern practice of polygamy) incorporating the essay's justifications.

Since I published the op-ed, I realized I made a mistake addressing the church. That's just not how change happens from the top. It was counter-productive, and nothing has changed. Since then Elder Dallin H. Oaks said the church doesn't give apologies, so me asking (however sincerely) for essayists to revise was naïve and will likely never happen.

Here's my revised ask. I'm asking for every parent and seminary teacher who reads this op-ed to carefully read through the seminary lesson and decide if they want youth to learn that God commanded Joseph to institute polygamy and marry teenagers and married women without Emma's knowledge. As you read, ask yourselves: Would a loving God do that to his children? Seminary teachers are instructed to walk students through the reasons God would command Joseph Smith and Abraham to practice polygamy (even though there's actually no mention in the Old Testament of God commanding Abraham. He just did it because polygamy was common practice among ancient nomadic tribes). The lesson's answer is, to raise righteous seed. It doesn't mention polygamy decreased the overall Mormon birthrate in early Utah. Sure, prominent polygamist men like Brigham Young had his posterity increased more than monogamous Mormon men — but his wives, along with other polygamous women, bore less children than they would have were they married monogamously.

The teacher then is to explain how polygamy was necessary because all ancient practices needed to be restored to complete the Church's Restoration. Joseph was just righteously doing what he was told, and he and those who practiced it with him were blessed for their obedience even though members first recoiled at idea.

Look, parents and teachers, sexual predators have been using these rationalizations to seduce girls long before the church recently published them. Study of this "deep doctrine" led many men, even a Utah teacher, to seduce teenagers under the premise that they were just following Joseph's example and had been similarly commanded of the Lord as righteous priesthood holders. Given that the current curriculum justifies the secrecy Joseph demanded of early followers of the practice, it's not hard to convince such victims that God is commanding them to keep their sexual behavior a secret until "the right time." This is Grooming 101.

When seminary instructors teach polygamy as God-commanded, justify Joseph's actions, read scripture verses as a class that treat women as property and bear testimony (as instructed) of these to Mormon youth worldwide, I cannot understate the psychological problems.

I've talked to a few parents and teachers about the curriculum's problematic aspects. Most are appalled. A few, however, surprisingly said to me that it's more important to follow the lesson manual as-is, do what they are told and pass responsibility for any consequences to those above them. I understand the perspective, but I strongly disagree on moral grounds and encourage everyone reading this to take a stand by following their conscience. You can teach the facts in the lesson without the spin. Instead of teaching "God commanded Joseph to institute polygamy," simply teach that Joseph Smith began practicing polygamy in the early 1830s. Play the clip of President Gordon B. Hinckley saying that he condemns polygamy because it's not doctrinal.

I guarantee you there are girls in your seminary class who are very uncomfortable reading in D&C 132 that if a man simply "desires a virgin," he has a God-given right to take her as a plural wife, and if he asks his first wife and she doesn't consent, he's free to take the virgin anyway. Better yet, ignore this lesson altogether and teach your students about Jesus Christ this Easter season.

Kristy Money is a psychologist and member of the board of Ordain Women.

Someone who perhaps had too much time on his hands—Apostle Orson Pratt

The Mormon Apostle Orson Pratt calculated how long the Mormon Mother-in-heaven was pregnant with the spirits of all the human beings who have been born on earth. He concluded it would have taken "over one hundred thousand millions of years for the same Mother to have given birth to this vast family." Orson Pratt, *The Seer*, March 1853, p. 38

<u>**Chapter Sixteen, WATER WORKS**</u>
According to "White Horse" oral prophecy of Joseph Smith Jr., Mormon elders will sweep in on a metaphorical white horse to save the day.

Joseph Smith's prophecy is explained in the *Encyclopedia of Mormonism:*

> LDS attachment to the Constitution has been further encouraged by an important oral tradition deriving from a statement attributed to Joseph Smith, according to which the Constitution would "hang by a thread" and be rescued, if at all, only with the help of the Saints. Church President John Taylor seemed to go further when he prophesied, "When the people shall have torn to shreds the Constitution of the United States the Elders of Israel will be found holding it up to the nations of the earth and proclaiming liberty and equal rights to all

men" (JD 21:8). To defend the principles of the Constitution under circumstances where the "iniquity," or moral decay, of the people has torn it to shreds might well require wisdom at least equal to that of the men raised up to found it. In particular, it would require great insight into the relationship between freedom and virtue in a political embodiment of moral agency. (1992, Vol. 1)

Brigham Young also commented on the prophecy:

> Brethren and sisters, our friends wish to know our feelings towards the Government. I answer, they are first-rate, and we will prove it too, as you will see if you only live long enough, for that we shall live to prove it is certain; and when the Constitution of the United States hangs, as it were, upon a single thread, they will have to call for the "Mormon" Elders to save it from utter destruction; and they will step forth and do it.

> We love the Constitution of our country; it is all we could ask; though in some few instances there might be some amendments made which would better it. (*Journal of Discourses*, February 18, 1855, Vol. 2, p. 182)

In 2006, however, Susan Easton Black, a BYU professor of Church history and doctrine, reportedly said that *"the prophecy as a whole is false"* ("White Horse in the White House," www.opinionjournal.com, November 3, 2006).

Also, on January 6, 2010, the LDS Church issued the following statement on its Newsroom blogsite: "The so-called 'White Horse Prophecy' is based on accounts that have not been substantiated by historical research and is not embraced as Church doctrine."

But the interest in Joseph's "oral prophecy" continues to increase, especially in view of presidential elections.

Chapter Eighteen, MOONLIGHT ON MERMAID TAILS

The patriarchal blessing

> Patriarchal blessings contemplate an inspired declaration of the lineage of the recipient, and also where so moved upon by the Spirit, an inspired and prophetic statement of the life mission of the recipient,

together with such blessings, cautions, and admonitions as the patriarch may be prompted to give for the accomplishment of such life's mission; it is always made clear that the realization of all promised blessings is conditioned upon faithful to the gospel of our Lord, whose servant the patriarch is. (Letter to all stake presidents dated June 28, 1957, from the First Presidency of the Church, David O.McKay, Stephen L. Richards, and J. Reuben Clark, Jr.)

Chapter Twenty-two, SINKHOLE OF FAITH

Joseph's Smith First Vision—complications with differing stories

Joseph Smith's Official First Vision Account written in 1838:

> Sometime in the second year after our removal to Manchester, there was in the place where we lived an unusual excitement on the subject of religion. It commenced with the Methodists, but soon became general among all the sects in that region of country ... and great multitudes united themselves to the different religious parties .... Some were contending for the Methodist faith, some for the Presbyterian, and some for the Baptist ... my mind became somewhat partial to the Methodist sect ... but so great were the confusion and strife among the different denominations, that it was impossible ... to come to any certain conclusion who was right, and who was wrong .... So in accordance with this, my determination to ask of God, I retired to the woods to make the attempt. It was on the morning of a beautiful, clear day, early in the spring of eighteen hundred and twenty ... I kneeled down and began to offer up the desires of my heart to God .... I saw a pillar of light exactly over my head .... When the light rested upon me I saw two Personages, whose brightness and glory defy all description .... One of them spake unto me, calling me by name and said, pointing to the other "This is My Beloved Son. Hear Him!" .... I asked the Personages who stood above me in the light, which of all the sects was right, (for at this time it had never entered into my heart that all were wrong) and which I should join. I was answered that I must join none of them, for they were all wrong ... I soon found, however, that my telling the story

had excited a great deal of prejudice against me among professors [believers] of religion, and was the cause of great persecution, which continued to increase; and though I was an obscure boy, only between fourteen and fifteen years of age ... yet men of high standing would take notice sufficient to excite the public mind against me, and create a bitter persecution; and this was common among all the sects all united to persecute me. (*Pearl of Great Price*, Joseph Smith - History 1:5-8, 14-19, 22)

This is where the interesting part begins, as there are several other accounts of the First Vision. The only one in Joseph Smith's own handwriting was written down about 1832, and does not refer to the Father and the Son appearing to him, but instead, Jesus. The account written in 1832 was never finished and was not accessible to the public until it was published in *BYU Studies,* Spring 1969, pp. 278ff. It also was included in Dean C. Jesse's *The Personal Writings of Joseph Smith* (1984, pp. 14ff).

There are substantial differences in the two versions. In the 1832 version, Joseph mentions that Jesus appeared to him, but in the 1838 rendition, he claimed that both the Father and the Son appeared.

More interesting, Joseph's own mother knew nothing about the Father and the Son appearing to him in the Sacred Grove. In her history, she tells of Mormonism beginning by an angel visiting Joseph in his bedroom (first draft of *Lucy Smith's History*, p. 46, LDS Church Archives). Now we're down from the Father and the Son, to Jesus, to one angel.

Then there's still another version. It was published in the periodical, *Latter-day Saints Messenger and Advocate* (Vol. 1, pp. 42, 78) in 1834. Joseph helped his scribe Oliver Cowdery write this account, and in this account he said, it was an angel, not Jesus, that appeared to him. And, like his mother said, this happened in his bedroom, not in a grove of trees.

So, depending on which version we read, it could have been a father and his son—God and Jesus? Mormon and his son Moroni (Book of Mormon prophets)?—or only Jesus, clear down to one angel that appeared to Joseph Smith. Two "personages," Jesus, or an angel— something most of us would remember.

Brigham Young even said specifically that the Lord did not visit young Joseph. As Brigham said, "The Lord did not come with the armies of heaven. But He did send His angel to this same obscure person, Joseph Smith jun ... and informed him that he should not join any of the religions of the day, for they were all wrong ..." (*Journal of Discourses* Vol. 2. p. 171).

A black hat is better than the Golden Plates—at least for translating scriptures.

> I will now give you a description of the manner in which the Book of Mormon was translated. Joseph Smith would put the seer stone into a hat, and put his face in the hat, drawing it closely around his face to exclude the light; and in the darkness the spiritual light would shine. A piece of something resembling parchment would appear, and on that appeared the writing. One character at a time would appear, and under it was the interpretation in English. Brother Joseph would read off the English to Oliver Cowdery, who was his principal scribe, and when it was written down and repeated to Brother Joseph to see if it was correct, then it would disappear, and another character with the interpretation would appear. Thus the Book of Mormon was translated by the gift and power of God, and not by any power of man. (David Whitmer, *A Witness To the Divine Authenticity of the Book of Mormon*, "An Address to All Believers in Christ," 1887, p. 12)

How many of Joseph Smith's plural wives were already married to other men when he married them?

"In fact, fully one-third of his [Joseph Smith's] plural wives, eleven of them were married to other men when he married them." (Todd Comptom, *In Sacred Loneliness: The Plural Wives of Joseph Smith*, 1997, pp. 15-16)

Chapter Twenty-three, TIDE'S A-CHANGING

Grant Palmer, a renowned LDS historian and author of *An Insider's View of Mormon Origins*, met with a general authority of the Mormon Church on March 26, 2013. Palmer quoted that general authority as follows:

> He [general authority] said that each new member of the Quorum of the Twelve Apostles is given one million dollars to take care of any financial obligations they have. This money gift allows them to fully focus on the ministry. He said that the overriding consideration of who is chosen is whether they are "church broke," meaning, will they do whatever they are told. He said the senior six apostles make the agenda and do most of the talking. (http://journeyofloyaldissent.wordpress.com/2013/04/06/6/)

The Church Mission Presidents Handbook is available online. Oh oh. Secret's out.

In December 2012, an official copy of the LDS Church's Mission President's Handbook, a publication not meant for the general public, was leaked. Now you can go to Google, type in "Mission President's Handbook," and voila!

> In Appendix B of this Mission President's Handbook, the Church discusses the financial advantages for the men presiding over its many missions across the world. The Church provides full reimbursement for the following expenses of the Mission President and his family while he serves his "unsalaried" three-year calling:
>
> 1. Medical expenses, including dental and eye care, though not orthodontics (except in specific cases) and cosmetic surgery (unless covered by the insurance provider);
>
> 2. Living Expenses, including rent, utilities, food, household supplies, utilities, telephone, Internet, dry cleaning, clothing for mission president and his family, family activities, long-distance personal phone calls, one round trip for each unmarried child under 26 if he/she did not accompany to the mission field, modest gifts (for example, Christmas, birthdays, or anniversary)

3. Education support for children serving full-time missions, elementary and secondary school expenses (including tuition, fees, books, and materials), expenses for extra-curricular activities for children such as music and dance lessons, undergraduate tuition at an accredited college or university (tuition cap at BYU's rate, tuition waived at Church-owned schools)

4. And, one part-time housekeeper/cook (20 hours/week), gardener if needed, one official car, with maintenance and gas provided for the mission president. The mission president's wife may use 'any mission vehicle available," with maintenance and gas provided.

Even more interesting direct quotes from the Mission President's manual.

The amount of any funds reimbursed to you should be kept strictly confidential and should not be discussed with missionaries, other mission presidents, friends, or family members.

TAX ISSUES

Because you are engaged in volunteer religious service, no employer-employee relationship exists between you and the Church. As a result, any funds reimbursed to you from the Church are not considered income for tax purposes; they are not reported to the government, and taxes are not withheld with regard to these funds.

To avoid raising unnecessary tax questions, please follow these guidelines closely:

Do not share information on funds you receive from the Church with those who help you with financial or tax matters. Any exceptions should be discussed with the Church Tax Division.

Never represent in any way that you are paid for your service.

If you are required to file an income-tax report for other purposes, do not list any funds you receive from the Church, regardless of where you serve or where you hold citizenship. (Mission President's Handbook, 2006, Appendices B, Family Finances, pp. 80-83, https://archive.org/

stream/MissionPresidentsHandbook2006/Mission%20Presidents_%20
Handbook-%282006%29#page/n1/mode/2up)

Don't Worry about the General Authorities, either.

See: http://www.dovesandserpents.org/wp/2013/01/how-much-does-
a-mormon-apostle-make/#sthash.IEszGOza.dpuf

Chapter Twenty-six, MUTINY

Coercion from on high

Letter from Elder Douglas L. Callister, Area Authority, to California
Stake Presidents,

May 20, 1999
To the Stake Presidents in California

Dear Brethren:

We are grateful for your willingness to support the request of the First
Presidency that we assist in every proper way to assure passage of the
Traditional Marriage Initiative ... This letter contains further instruc-
tions in connection with the raising of support funds as follows:

I have been asked to supervise the raising of the funds. I will be assisted
by Elders Merrill Higman and Floyd Packard. Within a few days one of
us will contact you.

In every instance the contribution of a Church member will be voluntary and in his capacity as a private citizen. No undue pressure of any
type will be applied.

No fundraising may take place on Church property, through use of
Church letterhead, or by virtue of general announcements in Church
meetings.

An education process will be required so that those approached will
understand that this is a moral issue, rather than political, fully justify-
ing the support of LDS families.

All checks should be made payable to "Defense of Marriage Committee" and mailed to Post Office Box 10637, Glendale, CA 91209-3637. We will keep appropriate accounting records and make these available to you for your individual stake. For each donor we need the name, address and occupation.

Please advise the donors that contributions are not tax-deductible.

We are pleased to accept contributions from any donor, whether or not a member of the Church. There is no limit on the amount of contribution, although any donor who contributes $10,000 or more must file a simple campaign report. (I can help with this.) We may also accept checks from businesses.

Experience shows that it is generally more successful to begin with the more affluent members, suggesting an appropriate contribution and thereafter extend the invitation to those of lesser means. We desire that as many as possible be invited to contribute in order to increase their awareness of the Initiative and develop a personal attachment to the project. Many of these members will be asked to provide telephone and other grass roots efforts near election time.

Our objective is to raise this money in 60-90 days.

We recognize that this is a large assignment. It is evidence of our continuing commitment to traditional families as the fundamental unit of society. Thank you for this and boundless other service you so faithfully offer.

Sincerely,
Douglas L. Callister
DLC/mj

The Gay and Lesbian Political Action Committee of Utah on Friday urged the LDS Church to halt its backing for an initiative that would ban same-sex marriage in California ... In a recent letter from top California church leaders, 740,000 members of The Church of Jesus Christ of Latter-day Saints in that state were encouraged to "do all you can by donating your means and time to assure a successful vote" on a ballot initiates that would deem only heterosexual marriages as "valid and recognized." (Gays Oppose LDS California Activism, *Salt Lake Tribune*, July 10, 1999)

DOMA overturned

On June 26, 2013, the Supreme Court overturned DOMA by declaring it unconstitutional.

Chapter Twenty-seven, FISHERS OF MEN
Keep your hands to yourself. No, no—that's not what I meant!

> While we should not regard this weakness [masturbation] as the heinous sin which some other sexual practices are, it is of itself bad enough to require sincere repentance. What is more, it too often leads to grievous sin, even to that sin against nature, homosexuality. For, done in private, it evolves often into mutual masturbation – practiced with another person of the same sex – and thence into total homosexuality. (Twelfth Prophet Spencer W. Kimball, *The Miracle of Forgiveness*, 1969, 27th printing, 1996, pp. 77 – 78)

This book is often required reading for a member seeking repentance for various sins.

No surprise—Mormon missionaries are mostly guys.

> As of 2007, 80% of all Mormon missionaries were young, unmarried men, 13% were young single women and 7% retired couples. Women who would like to serve a mission must meet the same standards of worthiness and be at least 21 years old; women generally serve shorter 18-month missions and are not actively encouraged to serve. (Peggy Fletcher Stack, "Mission metamorphosis," *The Salt Lake Tribune, June 30, 2007)*

Here is a big surprise: Retention rate of Church members reported at zero percent:

The convert retention rate for first generation Mormons is zero percent, according to a Peggy Stack's June 22, 2006 article, 'Keeping Members a Challenge for the LDS Church' that ran in the *Salt Lake Tribune*. (Read more at Suite 101: Low LDS Convert Retention Rate: The Growth of the Mormon Church Now Relies on People Born into Faith.)

Sociologist Armand Mauss stated that "75 percent of foreign [LDS] converts are not attending church within a year of conversion. In the United States, 50 percent of the converts fail to attend after a year." (Stacy A. Willis, "Mormon Church Is Funding Its Future," *Las Vegas Sun,* May 4, 2001)

And regarding the "Mormon Moment" . . .

USA Today
Why Mormons flee their church
Carrie Sheffield
June 17, 2012

The nation is having something of a "Mormon Moment." It is evident in unprecedented scrutiny of Mormon beliefs stemming from Mitt Romney's candidacy, the rise of social media, and a popular Broadway show and television programs. But largely overlooked is the growing reform movement within the Mormon community — one aimed at helping church leaders adapt to the modern world. They need help.

This year, Elder Marlin Jensen, the Mormon Church's outgoing official historian, acknowledged that members are defecting from the Church of Jesus Christ of Latter-day Saints "in droves" and that the pace is increasing.

(Continued at

Chapter Twenty-nine, FISHING AROUND

A few more damnable quotes—regarding the blacks

John Taylor, third president and prophet, wrote:

> ... after the flood we are told that the curse that had been pronounced upon Cain was continued through Ham's wife, as he had married a wife of that seed. And why did it pass through the flood? Because it was necessary that the devil should have a representation upon the earth as well as God ... (*Journal of Discourses*, Vol. 22, p. 304)
>
> But let them apostatize, and they will become gray-haired, wrinkled, and black, just like the Devil. (Brigham Young, *Journal of Discourses*, Vol. 5, p. 332)

American Indians are in the same cursed boat.

And it came to pass that I beheld, after they [American Indians] had dwindled in unbelief they became a dark, and loathsome, and a filthy people, full of idleness and all manner of abominations. (Book of Mormon, I Nephi 12:23)

> And he had caused the cursing to come upon them, yea, even a sore cursing, because of their [American Indians] iniquity ... wherefore, as they were white, and exceeding fair and delightsome, that they might not be enticing unto my people the Lord God did cause a skin of blackness to come upon them, (Book of Mormon, 2 Nephi 5:21)

The Book of Mormon states that when the Lamanites [American Indians] repented of their sins they became white like the Nephites [Caucasians from Jerusalem]. "And their curse was taken from them and their skin became white like unto the Nephites;" (Book of Mormon, 3 Nephi 2:15)

Chapter Thirty-one, BAILING

Early Church quotes referring to an angel—not God—appearing to Joseph

Brigham Young, second Mormon prophet:

> The Lord did not come with the armies of heaven ... But He did send his angel to this same obscure person, Joseph Smith jun., who afterwards became a Prophet, Seer, and Revelator, and informed him that he should not join any of the religious sects of the day, for they were all wrong. (*Journal of Discourses*, 1855, Vol. 2, p. 171)

Wilford Woodruff, fourth Mormon prophet:

> That same organization and Gospel that Christ died for, and the Apostles spilled their blood to vindicate, is again established in this generation. How did it come? By the ministering of an holy angel from God...The angel taught Joseph Smith those principles which are necessary for the salvation of the world...He told him the Gospel was not among men, and that there was not a true organization of His kingdom in the world ... This man to whom the angel appeared obeyed the Gospel ... (*Journal of Discourses* Vol. 2, pp. 196-197)

William Smith, Joseph's brother, remembered the vision as happening in 1823. He wrote that Joseph went into the woods to pray about which church to join. For a complete timeline, see http://www.utlm.org/onlineresources/firstvision.htm.

APPENDIX B

Symbolism—the Salt Lake Temple

From Matthew B. Brown and Paul Thomas Smith, "The Salt Lake Temple," in *Symbols in Stone: Symbolism on the Early Temples of the Restoration* (1997, pp. 117–156)

<u>Angel Moroni.</u> The angel Moroni depicts both a messenger of the restoration of the gospel and a herald of the Second Coming: 'for the Son of Man shall come, and he shall send his angels before him with the great sound of a trumpet, and they shall gather together the remainder of his elect from the four winds' (JS-M 1:37).

<u>Towers.</u> The three towers on the east side represent the First Presidency of the Church and the Melchizedek Priesthood; the twelve pinnacles rising from the towers represent the Twelve Apostles. The three towers on the west side represent the Presiding Bishopric and the Aaronic Priesthood; the twelve pinnacles rising from the towers represent the High Council.

<u>Battlements.</u> The castle-like battlements that surround the temple symbolize a separation from the world as well as a protection of the holy ordinances practiced within its walls.

<u>Earthstones.</u> The earthstones, located at the base of each buttress, represent the earth—the "footstool of God." Although the earth is currently a telestial kingdom, it will transition to a terrestrial kingdom at the coming of the Millennium; and at the end of one thousand years, it is destined to become a celestial kingdom.

Moonstones. Located directly above the earthstones, the moon is depicted in its various phases around the temple. The changing moon can represent the stages of human progression from birth to resurrection or represent the patron's journey from darkness to light.

Sunstones. Located directly above the moonstones, the sunstones depict the sun—a symbol of the glory of the celestial kingdom.

Cloudstones. High above the sunstones on the east center tower are two clouds with descending rays of light (originally planned to be one white and one black with descending trumpets.) The parallel of this symbolism is found in the Old Testament. Once temples were dedicated in ancient Israel, they were filled with the "cloud of the Lord." At Mount Sinai, the children of Israel saw this cloud as both dark and bright accompanied by the blasting of a trumpet.

Starstones. Six-pointed stars represent the actual stars in the heaven. Upside-down five-pointed stars represent morning stars, compared to the 'sons of God' in the scriptures. The large upright five-pointed stars may represent the governing power of the priesthood while the small upright five-pointed stars may represent the saving power of the priesthood for those who attach themselves to it.

Big Dipper. High on the west center tower is a depiction of the Big Dipper, a constellation used by travelers for thousands of years to find the North Star. It is an appropriate symbol for the temple where patrons come to get their bearings on the journey home.

Handclasp. Each of the center towers features a pair of clasped right hands identified as the 'right hands of fellowship' cited in Galatians 2:9. In Jeremiah 31:32, the Lord uses the handclasp to denote covenant making—an act at the very heart of temple worship.

All-Seeing Eye. Located atop each of the center towers of the temple is the all-seeing eye of God, which represents God's ability to see all things."

The all-seeing eye is also represented in the Celestial Room of the temple, and is a powerful Masonic symbol. Joseph Smith was a Master Mason.

Below is "The Family," the latest proclamation from the Church of Jesus Christ of Latter-day Saints, 1995. Their agenda ("marriage between a man and a woman is ordained of God") and timing (just before the vote on the Defense of Marriage Act), are clear. It was read by President Gordon B. Hinckley as part of his message at the General Relief Society Meeting held September 23, 1995, in Salt Lake City, Utah.

THE FAMILY
A Proclamation to the World

The First Presidency and Council of the Twelve Apostles of the
Church of Jesus Christ of Latter-day Saints

We, the First Presidency and the Council of the Twelve Apostles of The Church of Jesus Christ of Latter-day Saints, solemnly proclaim that marriage between a man and a woman is ordained of God and that the family is central to the Creator's plan for the eternal destiny of His children.

All human beings—male and female—are created in the image of God. Each is a beloved spirit son or daughter of heavenly parents, and, as such, each has a divine nature and destiny. Gender is an essential characteristic of individual premortal, mortal, and eternal identity and purpose.

In the premortal realm, spirit sons and daughters knew and worshipped God as their Eternal Father and accepted His plan by which His children could obtain a physical body and gain earthly experience to progress toward perfection and ultimately realize their divine destiny as heirs of eternal life. The divine plan of happiness enables family relationships to be perpetuated beyond the grave. Sacred ordinances and covenants available in holy temples make it possible for individuals to return to the presence of God and for families to be united eternally.

The first commandment that God gave to Adam and Eve pertained to their potential for parenthood as husband and wife. We declare that God's commandment for His children to multiply and replenish the earth remains in force. We further declare that God has commanded that the sacred powers of procreation are to be employed [leave it to Mormons to make sex sound like work] only between man and woman, lawfully wedded as husband and wife.

We declare the means by which mortal life is created to be divinely appointed. We affirm the sanctity of life and of its importance in God's eternal plan.

Husband and wife have a solemn responsibility to love and care for each other and for their children. "Children are an heritage of the Lord" (Psalm 127:3). Parents have a sacred duty to rear their children in love and righteousness, to provide for their physical and spiritual needs, and to teach them to love and serve one another, observe the commandments of God, and be law-abiding citizens wherever they live. Husbands and wives—mothers and fathers—will be held accountable before God for the discharge of these obligations.

The family is ordained of God. Marriage between man and woman is essential to His eternal plan. Children are entitled to birth within the bonds of matrimony, and to be reared by a father and a mother who honor marital vows with complete fidelity. Happiness in family life is most likely to be achieved when founded upon the teachings of the Lord Jesus Christ. Successful marriages and families are established and maintained on principles of faith, prayer, repentance, forgiveness, respect, love, compassion, work, and wholesome recreational activities. By divine design, fathers are to preside over their families in love and righteousness and are responsible to provide the necessities of life and protection for their families. Mothers are primarily responsible for the nurture of their children. In these sacred responsibilities, fathers and mothers are obligated to help one another as equal partners. Disability, death, or other circumstances may necessitate individual adaptation. Extended families should lend support when needed.

We warn that individuals who violate covenants of chastity, who abuse spouse or offspring, or who fail to fulfill family responsibilities will one day stand accountable before God. Further, we warn that the disintegration of the family will bring upon individuals, communities, and nations the calamities foretold by ancient and modern prophets.

We call upon responsible citizens and officers of government everywhere to promote those measures designed to maintain and strengthen the family as the fundamental unit of society.

About the Author

*F*or fifty years Lorelei lived the life of a devout Mormon woman.

As a child, her mother told her stories of her pioneer ancestors who crossed the plains to find religious freedom. She grew up in Salt Lake City, was baptized in the Tabernacle font on Temple Square, performed baptisms for the dead in the Salt Lake Temple, and also played the world-famous Tabernacle organ. She attended Brigham Young University, was sealed to her husband for time and all eternity in the Los Angeles Temple, and always said yes to the many callings her bishops extended to her.

Her life revolved around Mormonism and its clearly outlined path leading to exaltation. Then life's dilemmas thundered around her as she studied and prayed, and the doctrinal foundation she had built her life on crumbled.

She is a member of the California Writer's Club and a published poet. She's also named after a mermaid.

Made in the USA
Coppell, TX
09 March 2023

14003471R10146